W9-BMY-993

Tee Morris

Sams **Teach Yourself**

Twitter

in **10 Minutes**

800 East 96th Street, Indianapolis, Indiana 46240

Sams Teach Yourself Twitter in 10 Minutes

ISBN-13: 978-0-672-33124-4

ISBN-10: 0-672-33124-1

Library of Congress Cataloging-in-Publication data is on file.

Printed in the United States of America

First printing October 2009

Trademarks

All terms mentioned in this book that are known to be trademarks or service marks have been appropriately capitalized. Que Publishing cannot attest to the accuracy of this information. Use of a term in this book should not be regarded as affecting the validity of any trademark or service mark.

Warning and Disclaimer

Every effort has been made to make this book as complete and as accurate as possible, but no warranty or fitness is implied. The information provided is on an "as is" basis. The author and the publisher shall have neither liability nor responsibility to any person or entity with respect to any loss or damages arising from the information contained in this book.

Bulk Sales

Que Publishing offers excellent discounts on this book when ordered in quantity for bulk purchases or special sales. For more information, please contact

U.S. Corporate and Government Sales

1-800-382-3419

corpsales@pearsontechgroup.com

For sales outside of the U.S., please contact

International Sales

international@pearson.com

Associate Publisher
Greg Wiegand

Acquisitions Editor
Michelle Newcomb

Development Editor
Kevin Howard

Managing Editor
Patrick Kanouse

Project Editor
Seth Kerney

Copy Editor
Apostrophe Editing Services

Indexer
Ken Johnson

Proofreader
Williams Woods Publishing Services

Technical Editor
Philippa Ballantine

Publishing Coordinator
Cindy Teeters

Designer
Anne Jones

Compositor
Bronkella Publishing LLC

Contents

About the Author

Tee Morris has been an active member of the Twitter community since 2007 and part of the Social Media movement even longer. He established himself as a pioneer of podcasting by being the first to podcast a novel in its entirety. His fantasy epic, *MOREVI,* was a finalist for the 2006 Parsec Award for Best Podcast Novel. That production led to the founding of Podiobooks.com, the writing of *Podcasting for Dummies* (with Chuck Tomasi and Evo Terra), and the writing of *Expert Podcasting Practices for Dummies* (with Evo Terra and Ryan Williams). In 2009, he released his third Social Media-related title, *All a Twitter*, from Que Publishing. Tee has spoken across the country and around the world on Social Media for Book Expo America, Blogworld, CREATE South, Te Papa Tongarewa, and LIANZA. He is also the Social Media Manager for Intersections in Chantilly, Virginia.

Along with being a Social Media specialist, Tee is a columnist and critic for AppAdvice.com and writes Science Fiction and Fantasy found in print at Dragon Moon Press and in audio at TeeMorris.com. His fantasy-detective novel, *The Case of The Singing Sword: A Billibub Baddings Mystery*, received an Honorable Mention for *ForeWord* Magazine's 2004 Book of the Year award, was a Finalist for the 2005 Independent Publisher's Best Science Fiction and Fantasy, and won Best Audio Drama: Long Form at the 2008 Parsec Awards.

Find out more about Tee Morris at imaginethatstudios.com and teemorris.com on the Internet.

Photo by Kreg Steppe
(@steppek) of spyndle.com

Dedication

To those of you curious about Twitter, this book is your guide into getting in quick and discovering what the word on the Tweet is all about. Tweet unto others as you would have them tweet unto you, and have fun.

Acknowledgments

When I wrote *All a Twitter* earlier this year, I started off with *"What. A. Ride."* because I thought the ride had hit its stride, and I was closing in on the finish line....

Then I got a phone call asking me how quickly I could turn around *this* book. Good thing I was that kid who loved getting back in line for the roller coaster once I got out of the exit.

Unlike *All a Twitter* that is more commentary about Twitter, far-reaching in its scope and application, and involving more of the people who comprise the network, *Teach Yourself Twitter in 10 Minutes* is the bare-bones, fast-and-furious, breakneck crash course on Twitter. No case studies, no opinions and editorials, no personal anecdotes. Just the facts, ma'am. I have you for 10 minutes in each chapter, so I make it count.

I do need to thank my Google phone Goddess Annette Holland (@daNanner) and my BlackBerry banditos Matt Wilkins (@mattwilkins) and Denise Gideon (@bluearyn1) for their assistance with Twitter on platforms alien to me. I reached out and they offered their support. Not that their participation comes as a surprise to me. In fact, it's more of a testament to the power of a community and the potential Twitter has for everyone who uses it. At Twitter's core are people, and I consider myself most fortunate to be part of such a supportive community.

Welcome to Twitter.

We Want to Hear from You!

As the reader of this book, *you* are our most important critic and commentator. We value your opinion and want to know what we're doing right, what we could do better, what areas you'd like to see us publish in, and any other words of wisdom you're willing to pass our way.

As an associate publisher for Que Publishing, I welcome your comments. You can email or write me directly to let me know what you did or didn't like about this book—and what we can do to make our books better.

Please note that I cannot help you with technical problems related to the topic of this book. We do have a User Services group, however, where I will forward specific technical questions related to the book.

When you write, please be sure to include this book's title and author and your name, email address, and phone number. I will carefully review your comments and share them with the author and editors who worked on the book.

Email: feedback@quepublishing.com

Mail: Greg Wiegand
          Associate Publisher
          Que Publishing
          800 East 96th Street
          Indianapolis, IN 46240 USA

Reader Services

Visit our website and register this book at www.informit.com/title/ 9780672331244 for convenient access to any updates, downloads, or errata that might be available for this book.

Introduction

Welcome to Twitter, the Social Networking site that was called "utterly devoid of any sort of merit" by *New Zealand Herald's Canvas* Magazine, (June 6, 2009) in the same week it appeared on the cover of *TIME* Magazine as "a powerful form of communication" and "the future of American innovation." This lynchpin of the Social Media movement is loved by many, scrutinized by others; but in a nutshell, Twitter is a combination of instant messengers' immediacy, blogging's swiftness and spontaneity in reaching many with a message, and VoIP's capability to share and exchange media, and it does all this with a caveat that you must do this in 140 characters or less. This built-in limitation is your safeguard from Twitter becoming a timesink and a distraction. All these things have contributed to its incredible popularity and continue to make it all the talk both online and out in the real world.

This book explores what's out there, how to make it work, and gets you up and "tweeting" in record time.

Who Is Sams Teach Yourself Twitter in 10 Minutes For?

This intensive Twitter tutorial is designed for every level of user. *Teach Yourself Twitter in 10 Minutes* is geared for

- ▶ People who are starting from the beginning with Twitter
- ▶ Users who want to work beyond the Twitter.com homepage
- ▶ Users who want to incorporate images, audio, and video with their tweets
- ▶ Users who want to use Twitter with their smartphone
- ▶ Users experienced and new who are looking to build their networks

What This Book Covers

Twitter, in its amazing climb in notoriety, is more than the sum of its parts; and its first impression which, even *TIME* admits, isn't the best one. This book intends to take you into the wonderful world of Twitterspeak while, at the same time, give you a complete and in-depth overview (albeit, in 10 minute chunks) of what you can do.

Teach Yourself Twitter in 10 Minutes begins with setting up an account. Although this might seem self-explanatory, many of the basic mistakes with Twitter start here. From viewing the Twitter homepages of others to making sure your profile is complete, you are given tricks and tips that can help you make the best of first impressions.

From establishing your Twitter account, you are then introduced to the art of tweeting. (Yes, we really do call it *tweeting* when you post an update or talk from one user to another.) We start with the most basic of tweets— composing a tweet and turning on your internal editor to stay under the 140-character limits—and build on these skills to incorporate URLs. We also go into various ways you can track trends and traffic using hashtags, URL shorteners, and a variety of search engines. We then go into sharing media, such as still images, audio, and video, through a variety of online utilities geared to extend Twitter's capabilities.

Next, *Teach Yourself Twitter in 10 Minutes* takes users away from their Twitter.com homepage and looks at third-party applications. The desktop clients featured are best for accounts managing small and large networks, and their basic steps of installation and operation can easily be adapted to other desktop clients, both currently available and yet-to-come. Then we take Twitter on the go, featuring applications for the G1, BlackBerry, and iPhone. These applications bring all the features you are introduced to in previous chapters to your smartphones, bringing the Twitter experience anywhere you are.

Finally, we take a closer look at building and cultivating a network using everything from previously discussed Search engines to online services designed to evaluate, organize, and encourage growth in your followers. Keep in mind—this title is composed of tutorials, so there is little in the way of case study, advice, and commentary on "what makes a network strong." For tutorials and tips of a more theoretical and practical nature, check out my other title, *All a Twitter*, from Que Publishing, featuring chapters like "Going Pro with Twitter," "ANTI-Social Media," and "Why I Twitter."

What You Need to Use This Book

Apart from a computer, whether it's a desktop or laptop model, with an Internet connection or a smartphone with a data connection, all that you actually need for this book is a genuine curiosity concerning Twitter. If you are not even slightly curious as to how this works, what you can do with it, and why you need to figure it out, this trip into the Twitterverse might be a rough one. Curiosity is one of the driving forces of Twitter. After all, it got developers thinking, "If I can send messages like this, I wonder if..." and from there we now have online services such as 12seconds.tv, TwitPic, and MobyPicture.

Along with curiosity, you also need time. Obviously, I have 10-minute blocks to teach you something, sure; but the time I refer to is the time to build a network and establish your community. Contrary to popular belief of self-proclaimed Social Media gurus, oracles, mavens, and experts, communities do not build themselves overnight with automated services. Real communities are based on communication, participation, and relationships, and these kinds of communities take time to cultivate. *Teach Yourself Twitter in 10 Minutes* can give you the tools on how to do that. That, I can teach you in 10 minutes. However, you can't build a community in 10 minutes. Your network requires time. Not a large amount of time, but time and attention to achieve its potential.

What to Expect from Here

Throughout the book you find a few callouts that serve as convenient tips and must-know tricks to make the most of your Twitter experience.

Notes

These bits of advice range from interesting background trivia to truly cool options you might miss in desktop clients and mobile applications if you blink at the wrong time. These are the Easter Eggs of Twitter that you need to know.

Warnings

Throughout *Teach Yourself Twitter in 10 Minutes*, Warnings are the pitfalls and networking faux pas many new users (and even some experienced ones) make while tweeting. Tempting as it is to simply jump in and figure things out as you go, the Warnings are there to make sure common mistakes are avoided, protocols are protected, and etiquette (or *Twittiquette*) is upheld.

Beyond Teach Yourself Twitter in 10 Minutes

Keeping books on anything involving your computer up-to-date has evolved from a tricky task to a Herculean task to "just frakking insane." Between signing off *All a Twitter* and writing *Teach Yourself Twitter in 10 Minutes*, here's what happened just within a month:

- ▶ Several upgrades for TweetDeck, Twittelator Pro, and other popular applications. (And in a word, WOW! Many of the updates are covered in this book.)

- ▶ Twitter's deal with Vodophone to offer to its New Zealand customers full, two-way SMS. (And the kiwis got it *before* Australia!)

- ▶ The Twitpocalypse (which wound up to be a lot of hype...)

- ▶ Several redesigns at Twitter.com. (I love the new look of the Followers and Following pages.)

- ▶ The aforementioned *TIME* Magazine cover story. (Congrats @biz, @ev, and @twitter!)

▶ The Iranian election protest (resulting in green avatars everywhere)

And, no doubt, a lot of things can happen between now and the time this book reaches you. So how do I compete with the books that are about to hit the shelves or compare to the books currently on the shelves?

Simple answer: I don't stop. The book might conclude at the closing of its cover, but the lessons, assistance, and insight continues online through a variety of outlets.

Social Media Specialist on Call (via Twitter)

Of course, you can find me on Twitter, and of course, I would be more than happy to answer your questions concerning Twitter. If you find yourself stuck or curious as to what to try next, go on and drop me a tweet at @ITStudios (for Imagine That! Studios), and I will reply when the tweet arrives. Feel free to also share with me feedback, both the congratulatory and the critical, on *Teach Yourself Twitter in 10 Minutes*. Twitter is all about reaching out and connecting, and I'm out there if you have a question for me. (And when you do tweet me concerning this title, use the hashtag #twitterin10. Hashtags. in Chapter 4. Check them out!)

Imagine That! Studios

Imagine That! Studios (http://imaginethatstudios.com) is my online home in which I discuss creative solutions in the workplace. Through Social Media, audio and video production, and clever thinking, solutions are discovered. That's my mantra there. If you are looking for additional resources or commentary concerning Social Media, you might find what you need at Imagine That! Studios. Come on by, take a look around, and enjoy what my blog has to offer.

Bird House Rules

Finally, there is the official blog and podcast of *All a Twitter* and *Teach Yourself Twitter in 10 Minutes*, found at http://twitterin10.com. This 10-minute podcast picks up where the book leaves off, keeping the content you find here current and up-to-date. The podcast is a handy audio addendum to this book and your chance to put a voice with the tweets; the RSS feed also features interviews and audio and video clips from interviews concerning the book and Twitter. The blog offers commentary, guest postings, and topics generated by you, the new and experienced Twitter user. Have a listen and a read, or subscribe through iTunes or your RSS reader of choice.

LESSON 1

Introducing Twitter

Twitter first went online in 2006 and in the three years has become the essential tool to introduce Social Media in business. For the casual user, Twitter is also an essential tool as it bridges the gap between blogging and instant messaging. Regardless if the reason behind your interest is for personal or professional application, Twitter's popularity can be attributed back to its initial ease of use.

When you get past Twitter's initial learning curve of communication, there is more. Much more. Sure, you can learn the basics in 10 minutes (just as the title promises), but why stop there? On the surface, Twitter appears to be nothing more than a variation on Facebook's Status Update feature. The potential and power of Twitter, as well as how it is different from Facebook, comes from how you build your network and then engage your community with what you are doing at that particular moment. What might seem to be "just another day" to you is your network's sneak peek into your creative process or what you are accomplishing. Whether it is "working out a tricky plot snag between two characters" or "sitting down with the CEO on outlook for 2009," this is an inside perspective that interests your followers.

If you have never hosted a blog, Twitter is a fantastic primer in doing so. Sometimes referred to as *microblogging*, Twitter is the sharing of your thoughts or actions at that particular moment, much like a blog post. One difference from blogs is that your thoughts appear as a posting at http://twitter.com. A major difference between true blogs and Twitter, though, is that in Twitter your thoughts must be composed within 140 characters (including spaces) or less. This limitation makes you pare down your posting (or *tweet*) to the basics. When you send out a tweet, those in your network (your *Followers*, which are listed by their avatars in a grid on the main page of your Twitter account) see it. That is Twitter: your personal quick response network.

FIGURE 1.1   Twitter takes your thoughts in brief 140-character-sized blog posts and distributes them across your own network.

Viewing a Twitter Homepage

Even without being registered on Twitter, you can view individual Twitter streams. These are previous tweets made by whomever you review through your browser. What you need to know is the user's (or *Twitter* as I refer to them. You might hear others call users *Tweeters*, as well) name on the network.

1. Go to http://twitter.com on your Internet browser. This takes you to the Sign In/Join Twitter homepage.

   We return to this in a later exercise. For now, focus your attention to the URL field in your browser.

2. Just after http://twitter.com in your browser's URL field, enter in a username. Examples of a username can include

   ITStudios

   TeeMonster

Enter in a username of a Twitter you would like to review. After the URL looks like http://twitter.com/ITStudios, press Enter on your keyboard.

3. Your browser is now directed to the user's Twitter homepage. You can now scroll along his or her timeline of tweets, beginning with the most recent and continuing farther back.

NOTE

When viewing people's timeline, take a look at how they participate on Twitter. How do they engage their network? Do they use Twitter as a microblog? Do they reply to members of their network? Do they share and circulate various online resources? Or are they doing all the above? Reviewing a user's timeline provides valuable insight into the character of that Twitter and how he or she regards their network.

---

4. To view more in a user's timeline, simply scroll to the bottom of the tweets and single-click the More button. This loads up more tweets into the browser window.

This is actually all there is to reviewing a user's timeline. Without an account, the communication is a one-way street with you merely on the receiving end of the Twitter feed. Go on and surf to other users' homepages. Take a look at how these people use Twitter.

NOTE

Direct Messages are more personal exchanges between you and another Twitter user following you. We cover them later in Lesson 3, "Communicating with Others on Twitter," but note that your Direct Messages (or DMs) never appear in the **public** timeline. These are tweets for your eyes and the eyes of the sender/recipient only.

When you have an idea of how people tweet between one another, consider your message and what you would like to say because we are now about to create a Twitter account.

Setting Up a Twitter Account

What I define here as "setting up an account" is simply signing up. This is when most new users make their first mistake: They set up the account and they consider themselves "done" when this is merely the first step. To those who immediately tweet after this step I applaud your zeal and vigor for wanting to engage right away; but before you start building your network, stop for a moment and consider the details of your account.

To attract followers and effectively build a network, you need to go deeper into establishing a presence on Twitter. In Lesson 2, "Completing Your Profile," we complete an online profile, create an avatar for our account, and then seek out other Twitters that share common interests.

Let's begin with the basics to register on Twitter.

1. Go to http://twitter.com on your Internet browser.

2. To the right of the search button is a button reading "Sign Up Now." Single-click that button.

3. In the field marked Full Name, type in your full name or your business' name, or both.

> **NOTE**
>
> Honesty is the best policy when building your profile, so don't be shy or elusive here. A real or company name can better help you in establishing an identity on Twitter. You can, at any time under Settings, change your full name to something different, be it to one for personal or professional use.

4. Set up a User Name, no longer than 15 characters (Twitter's built-in limit). This can be your nickname, a clever wordplay, or your organization's name or acronym.

> **WARNING**
>
> When creating usernames, keep your monikers simple. When people reply to your tweets, your name counts as characters used. You can use underscores in lieu of spaces, but again consider how easy it is to type your Twitter ID. Additionally, avoid using numbers and a random mix of uppercase letters in your usernames because these traits can alert Twitter's security measures. Many spammers use auto-generated names such as Darrin1234 and InDigOgRRls, for example. Be clever, sure; but keep it easy.

5. Create your password.

Along with letting you know if a full name is "too big" or a username is available, Twitter also evaluates your password, rating it between *strong* or *weak*. Strong passwords usually are a mix of uppercase and lowercase letters with numbers used in place of certain alphabetical characters. When you come up with a password, make it something easy to remember but not easy for others to figure out.

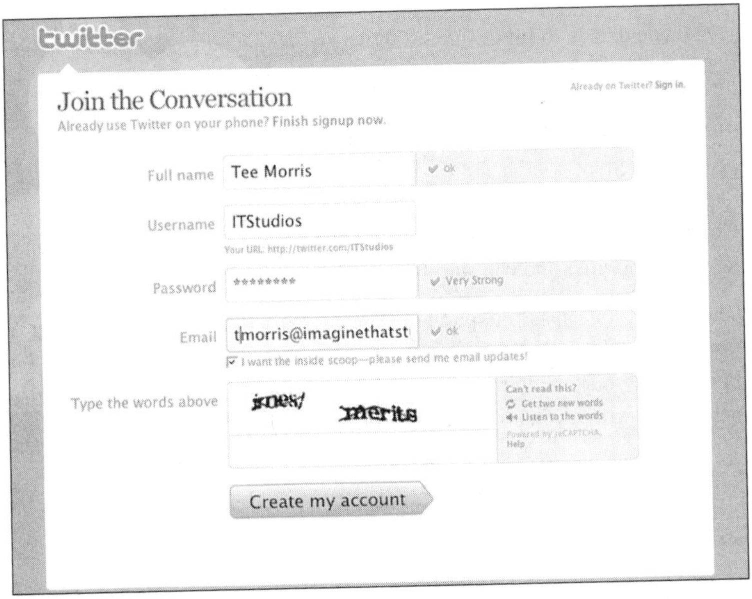

FIGURE 1.2   Your Twitter account begins with the basics: who you are, where Twitter can contact you, and what is your password.

6. If you want to be notified of new followers and when people send you direct messages, check the box for email updates.

7. In the final field, type the verification code provided by Twitter. If you cannot read the code, you can refresh the verification by single-clicking on the Get Two New Words option or hear an audio version of the verification code by single-clicking on the Listen to the Words link, both located to the right of the field.

8. Single-click Create My Account to finish registration.

9. Following the creation of your Twitter account, Twitter offers you the option to check email directories for any friends you think might be on Twitter. If you choose any of these featured services, have your own user details for your mail accounts ready to enter. Single-click "Skip This Step" if you wish to progress to the next screen.

10. In this option, Twitter selects at random a variety of Twitter users you can start following straight away. This cross-section of Twitters can include celebrities, organizations, frequent Twitters, or Twitter accounts often referenced or retweeted by others. If you decide to follow any of these Twitter accounts, click on the check boxes located to the left of their accounts, and then single-click on Finish at the bottom of the interface. If you do not want to follow any of these suggested accounts, single-click on Skip This Step.

Congratulations! If your browser looks like Figure 1.3, you are now registered with Twitter and can start tweeting straight away.

This is everyone's starting point on Twitter. With these simple details set, you can now begin building your own network of followers, let them know what your are doing in that moment, and even provide exact coordinates as to where you are tweeting from, and vice versa.

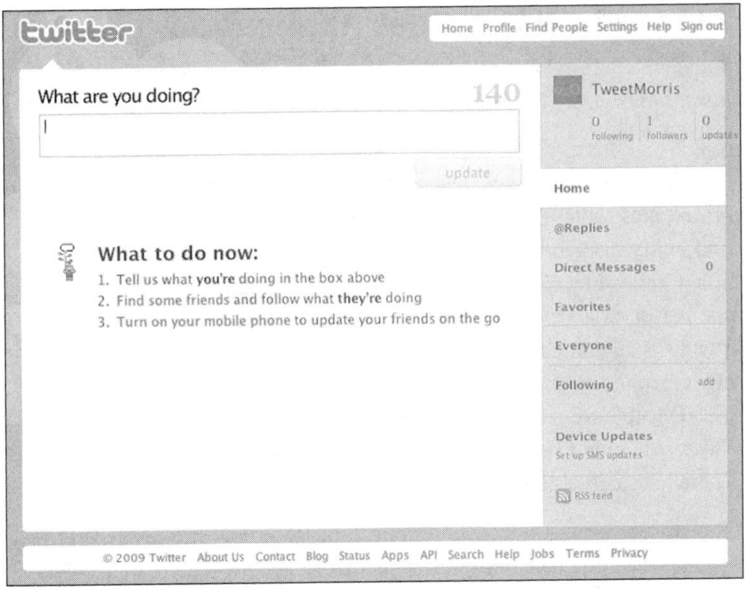

FIGURE 1.3 New Twitter accounts display a default avatar against Twitter's default background, a username, and tips on building a network.

Tempting as it is to simply say, "Let's start tweeting...", now would be a good time to remind you what I said earlier: many of the mistakes and misconceptions of Twitter happen here. Before we even go into the completion of your profile, we should take a moment to go into exactly what Twitter is not. With its recent explosion of popularity, many jump into Twitter with preconceived notions and either walk away disappointed or participate disillusioned.

Let's take a few moments to look at Twitter with a more critical eye.

What Twitter Is Not

Twitter, I believe, is the Swiss Army Knife of Social Media, considering all its capabilities and possibilities; but where Twitter fails is when new users believe it is something that it is not.

Twitter Is Not a Chat Application

Some are confused and upset when they discover that Twitter is not an *Instant Messenger* (or *IM*) or try to use it as an IM application with one wicked delay!

In some ways Twitter does resemble an application like *Skype, AOL Instant Messenger (AIM), iChat,* or the various chat add-ons you might find in MySpace or Facebook, but it was never meant to be a chat application. Replies in a chat application are usually private and kept between one person or a group of invited individuals. Your tweet exchange on Twitter is automatically shared across a network. In other words, this is not a private conversation you are having. Everyone is invited. You can use DMs to have private conversations, but this is another reason why Twitter shouldn't be considered a true chat application or used as such: There is usually a long delay before you get an answer.

The most obvious reason Twitter fails as an IM application is its strongest feature: the 140-character limitation. This safeguard is there to keep your communication to the basics. If you cannot keep a single statement within one (or two) tweets, it's time to move the talk to Skype, iChat, or Facebook Chat.

Twitter Is Not a Blog

Although I do consider Twitter as "a test drive for potential bloggers," Twitter is not a blog. True, Twitter does use RSS feeds to enable your tweets for the day to appear as a blogpost. True, Twitter asks you what you are doing at that very moment. True, people follow you much in the same way that people subscribe to your blog.

Twitter can do all this, just like a blog—but it's not a blog.

Blogs usually follow a theme or (if they are of a more personal nature) a variety of subjects. Twitter covers everything including the kitchen sink and depending on the person tweeting, things you would never want to do in, on, or anywhere *near* the kitchen sink! Following a single topic in Twitter can be a bit challenging. It's possible but limited to how much you can say about the topic at hand. Additionally, you can reply and comment on a topic in Twitter; but if a week later, you want to return to that original tweet, you would find that a challenge because you would need to weed through a week's worth of tweets before finding it. Then you would have to bring others in your network up to speed on exactly what you are talking about. With blogs, you have posts categorized and organized, and always with a reference point that its comments continuously reference.

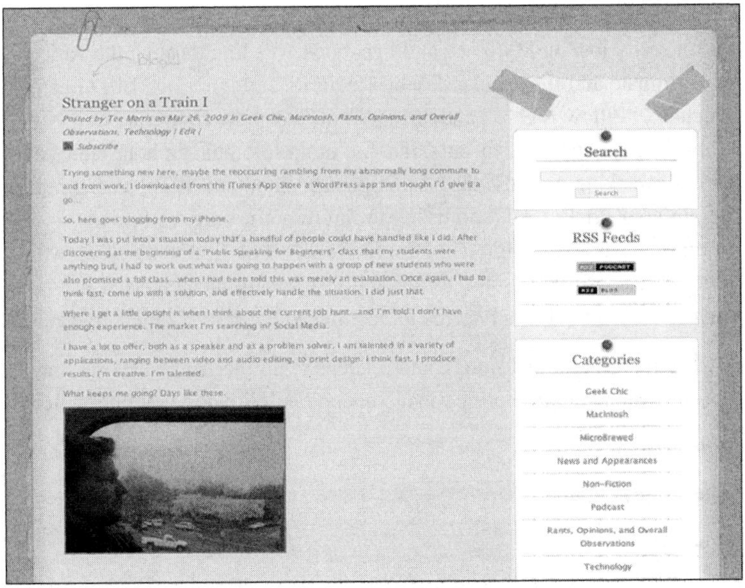

FIGURE 1.4 Blogposts like this one, although Twitter can provide links to them, would be impossible (or downright annoying) to display through a series of tweets.

Also, blogposts can be 140 words or, if the blogger is particularly passionate, *1,400* words. Blogposts can also feature images, audio, and video whereas Twitter provides only reference links. Twitter might behave like a blog in many ways, but is far from it. You can use Twitter as a blog (and many users choose to do so), and this is how it serves as a nice primer for blogging. If you find Twitter a lot of fun, check out *WordPress* (http://wordpress.com) or a similar blog host. Within minutes you can have a true weblog up and running, and with a few clicks you can even have a plug-in that automatically tweets for you when your latest blogpost goes live.

Twitter Is Not Like Facebook, MySpace, or Other Social Networks

"I really don't have the time for Twitter."

This is probably the biggest excuse I hear from people on why they are not giving Twitter a shot. Where is this coming from? Could it be the hours of productivity lost on MySpace and Facebook weeding through the variety of legitimate and illegitimate Friend Requests and ignoring "Li'l Green Patches," "Pillow Fights," and "Mob Wars"? Or how about, in Ning Communities, there are discussions you jump into; and an hour later you are still working on those discussion posts? Whether it is approving others to join your Flickr feed (and trying to figure out if they are Friends, Friends & Family, or simply a "Contact") or if you find yourself drawn into a thread appearing on a forum you just joined, the perceived investment of time into Twitter seems to be a major barrier for others to clear.

Twitter took that into account, and it keeps it simple. You have only three options when you are notified that someone is following you on Twitter:

▶ Follow

▶ Not Follow

▶ Block

Twitter is the definition of low maintenance. Perhaps, if you want to delete previous tweets or drop followers, the Twitter.com interface does not lend itself to user-friendly actions. You cannot Select All of previous tweets and press a Delete key, and you cannot easily search out Twitter users in your network. However, building your network takes only a few minutes. How deep your involvement with your Twitter network falls back on you and the parameters you set. Twitter becomes high maintenance only if you allow it to be.

So, are you all set up and ready to tweet? Well, not quite. Although you can begin building up your network, connecting with others, and embracing this hot new Social Networking initiative, let's stop a moment and consider those two words: *Social Networking*. It's all about the first impression, isn't it? When making contacts and creating a network—even the virtual ones— it is imperative to put your best foot forward.

This is what we do with a completed Twitter profile.

LESSON 2

Completing Your Profile

To attract followers and effectively begin building your network, you need to go deeper into establishing a presence on Twitter. We will do so by completing our online profile, giving some serious thought behind what our profile picture will be, and seeking out other Twitter users that share common interests with us.

If you skipped the opportunities in your initial setup to follow other Twitters, no one is following you at present. Your Twitter page is empty and your avatar appears as "O_o" which serves as your default Twitter picture. From this universal starting point, we will begin building that network; but first, let's fill in our user profile. These seemingly small details are essential in making that lasting first impression a positive one.

Your Display Name

Your username, Twitter's default option, is currently displayed. For many users, this works fine but you can give users more than just an online nickname. You are introducing yourself. This is how people will see you in their Twitter clients (two such clients are described in detail in Chapters 6, "Using Third-Party Applications: Twhirl," and 7, "Using Third-Party Applications: TweetDeck").

When you decide the best way for people to identify you on Twitter, take a few moments to edit your display name.

  1. Log into Twitter (if you haven't already) and when your home-page (found at http://twitter.com/home) loads, click on the Settings option, located at the top of the page.

  2. In the Name field, you can set up your real name, nickname, company moniker, or your own moniker-of-the-day.

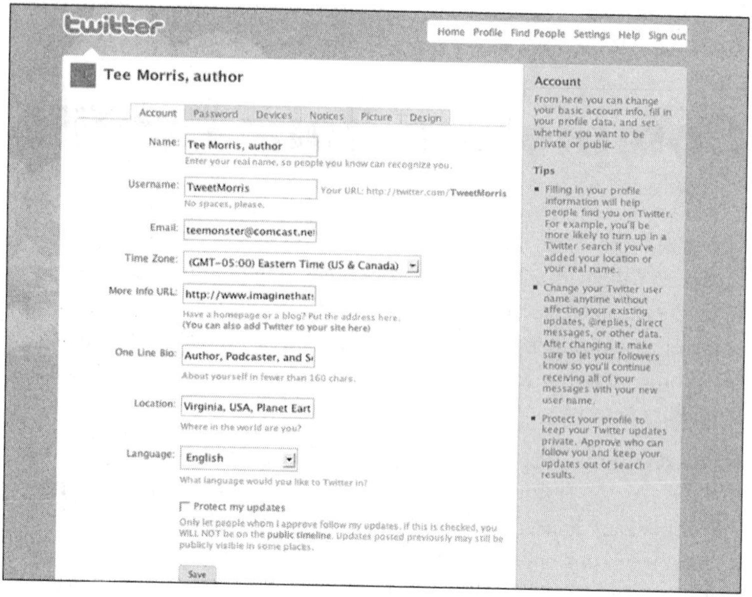

FIGURE 2.1   At the top of your Twitter homepage are options for your Twitter account. Settings is where you can customize and adjust your Twitter presence to fit your mood or intent.

NOTE

When coming up with your name, Twitter allows 20 characters. That includes spaces.

---

3. In the Username field, you see the identity you logged in with. Although you can change this, it is best to stay with the one you originally created, for simplicity's sake. Same goes for the email address, unless you decide to give your Twitter account a complete makeover, which you can do here.

You have a new name in place, but note there are still a few more details remaining for your Twitter profile. These details will take only a few minutes to complete.

Additional Profile Information

Now that you have introduced yourself, let's add to this first impression with details that give Twitter users everywhere an idea of where you tweet from and where people can find out more about you outside of Twitter.

1. In the Time Zone field, select your current time zone. This assists Twitter in rendering accurate time stamps appearing in your tweets and details that other clients report to their users.

2. More Info URL is where you enter a website, personal or professional, that best represents you. The URL should give people a more detailed background than what they would find on Twitter.

3. In the One Line Bio field, enter in a message, personal tagline, or quote that best describes you to the world. Twitter limits what you can say here to 160 characters or less.

4. In the Location field, enter in where you are in the world. This can be a literal location, a state of mind, or (for some Twitter users) coordinates from Google Maps.

5. If you tweet in a different language, you can change your dialect in the Language drop-down menu.

NOTE

The remaining options under Language are security options: Protect My Updates and Delete My Account, covered later in this chapter.

---

6. Single-click on Save to save your changes.

7. When your changes have been verified, click on the Profile option at the top of the screen to take a look at your profile in progress.

With these details covered, you have already improved your introduction to others on Twitter.

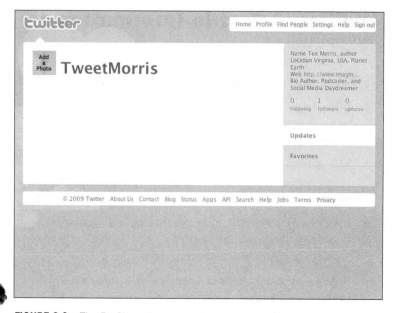

FIGURE 2.2   The Profile option in the Twitter menu gives you a look at how your page appears to others in Twitter and displays your public tweets and replies independent of other tweets in your network.

You might also see, as depicted in Figure 2.2, a small icon to the left of your username that Twitter is making a suggestion: Add a Photo. That small icon is also known as an avatar, a common trait found in many Social Media initiatives. The avatar might seem like a tiny detail, but it can carry the same impact as a name, bio, and accompanying URL.

The Importance of a Good Avatar

The icon you create for Twitter becomes (to coin a marketing term) your personal brand on Twitter. When using Twitter for business, it stands to reason that your company's logo (used with permission, of course) serves as your avatar. With your own personal account, your avatar can be just about anything you want it to be, and often users will within a few clicks switch out their avatars to reflect what kind of a day, week, or life they are having. The avatar takes the "What are you doing?" aspect of Twitter to a visual level.

Creating an Avatar with iPhoto

It is difficult to talk about avatars if you don't know how to make one, and there are many kinds of photo editors out there. In *Teach Yourself Twitter in 10 Minutes*, we take a closer look at three different editors available for Macintosh and Windows operating systems. Two of these editors come pre-installed in your operating systems whereas the third one is Adobe's powerhouse of digital photography.

Right now, I'm going to focus on iPhoto, one of the applications bundled with Apple's iLife (http://www.apple.com/ilife) and pre-installed on new Macintosh computers. It is a simple and basic photo editor and a snap to use. For Mac users out there, this is how you go about creating an avatar.

1. Open up a window in the Finder and under Applications, launch iPhoto.

2. Click on File > Import to Library (Shift+Command+I), and from your Pictures folder or a folder of your own creation, find a photograph you want to use for your avatar. It can be the whole photo or a part of it.

3. When the image appears in your iPhoto library, double-click on it to access iPhoto's editing feature.

4. Single-click the Edit button (a pencil) and then single-click the Crop tool. You can now click-and-drag the corners of the cropping area to select only what you want from the photo.

5. From the Crop Options bar near the bottom of the image, click Apply to crop the photo.

6. With the photo cropped, go to File > Export and select a format for your new avatar, and single-click the Export button.

> **NOTE**
> Avatars should be saved in either JPEG or PNG formats. You can use GIFs but their resolution tends to be poor quality compared to JPEGs or PNGs.

7. Give your image a name and then save it on your Desktop (so that it will be easy to find).

FIGURE 2.3   In iPhoto, you can create terrific avatars from larger photographs by using the Crop tool.

Creating an Avatar with Windows Photo Gallery

For Windows Vista users, the Windows Photo Gallery is your pre-installed solution to create the best avatar for your Twitter account. Like iPhoto, the Photo Gallery keeps it simple and basic, and can produce an avatar ready in only a few ticks of the clock and clicks of a mouse.

1. Go to the Windows icon in the lower-left corner of your Window and single-click. From the All Programs option, find Windows Photo Gallery.

2. Click on File > Import from Camera or Scanner, or Add Folder to Gallery to bring in your photographs. From your gallery (current or recently created), find a photograph you want to use for your avatar.

3. Double-click on a photo and then select Fix from the Gallery's menu to access the Photo Gallery editing features.

4. Single-click the Crop Picture button and then drag the corners of the cropping area to select only what you want from the photo, as shown in Figure 2.4.

FIGURE 2.4 Windows Vista offers its users the Windows Photo Gallery to create an avatar that best represents who they are in the Twitterverse.

5. Single-click the Apply button to crop the photo.

6. With the photo cropped, go to File > Make a Copy and select a format for your new avatar and single-click the Save button.

> **NOTE**
> Avatars should be saved in either JPEG or PNG formats. You can use GIFs but their resolution tends to be poor quality compared to JPEGs or PNGs.

7. Give your image a name and then save it on your Desktop (so that it will be easy to find).

iPhoto and Photo Gallery are cost-free (in most cases) options you have to create avatars; but when it comes to working with digital photography, editing photographs, and creating eye-popping images, Adobe's Photoshop (http://adobe.com/photoshop) remains a standard for photographers both amateur and commercial. Photoshop not only is a powerful imaging tool but also runs on both Macintosh and Windows platforms.

Creating an Avatar with Photoshop

If you have access to Photoshop, you can tend to a few more details when creating your avatar; these details can improve downloading time for both Twitter and third-party clients.

1. Open up a window in the Finder and under Applications, launch Photoshop.

2. Click on File > Open (Command+O for Mac, Control+O for Windows), and from your Pictures folder or a folder of your own creation, find a photograph you want to use for your avatar. It can be the whole photo or a part of it.

3. When Photoshop opens the image, from Tools single-click the Crop tool.

4. Place the Crop tool at the center of your desired avatar image. Click-and-hold your primary mouse button down, and then hold down the Shift+Option (Mac) or the Shift+Alt keys. Click-and-drag the Crop tool to constrain movement and create a cropping area from the center of your origin point.

5. Double-click inside the cropping area or go to Image > Crop to crop the photo.

6. After the photo is cropped, go to Image > Image Size and double-check to make certain the Resolution is set at 72 pixels/in or 28.3 pixels/cm.

7. If needed, resize the image to 600 pixels in width. (Height should automatically match the width provided you followed step 4 with the keyboard options and the Constrain Proportions option is checked.) Click OK after you adjust the image.

8. Go to Image > Mode and make sure that RGB is checked. If it is not, select RGB as the image's color mode.

9. Select File > Export to Web, select a format for your new avatar, and single-click the Save button.

FIGURE 2.5 Photoshop can create a perfectly proportioned avatar with its Crop tool and a few keyboard shortcuts.

NOTE

Avatars you create in Photoshop should be saved in either JPEG or PNG formats. Additionally, images should be in RGB color mode, 72 pixels/in in resolution and 600 x 600 pixels (or smaller) in size.

---

10. Give your image a name and then save it on your Desktop (so that it will be easy to find).

When creating an avatar, consider that impression you want to make. Is this a professional impression you want to make, or are you introducing yourself with a sense of humor? Find the image that is your best representation and then make the image Twitter-friendly through one of the preceding exercises.

WARNING

Some Twitter users have employed Animated GIFs as avatars. Although using GIFs is a viable option, animated avatars tend to be harsh reminders of annoying chat room and forum artwork. Animated avatars are also inconsistent. They work fine on Twitter homepages but fail with many third-party applications and mobile devices.

Animated avatars, in the end, are eyesores and scream of amateurish web design. The best option is to avoid them at all costs.

Incorporating an Avatar for Twitter

With the avatar now ready to go, let's swap out the default image for our own customized image.

1. Click on the Settings option at the top of your Twitter interface, and then single-click on the Picture tab.

2. Currently displayed to the left of the blank data field is your current avatar. Single-click Browse to search through your computer for an avatar that best represents you, your business, or your current mood. (The avatar you created earlier in this chapter is on your computer's Desktop.)

3. When you find the image you want to use as an avatar, select it and then click OK.

4. Single-click on the Save button.

5. You receive confirmation that the avatar is in place when you see That's a Nice Picture along the top. (This message disappears after a few seconds.)

NOTE

If you have difficulty using an image for Twitter, or still are not sure what makes a good avatar, take a look at the suggestions from Twitter under the Picture bar along the right side of the page. You can get a few helpful hints on what to consider or what could be causing the problems with uploading the image.

6. Single-click on Profile and then click on the image. Twitter shows you the image at its full size with the Name you entered.

FIGURE 2.6 When a new avatar is in place, Twitter renders it in your Profile full size for potential followers to see.

Customizing Twitter

Right now, your profile is complete, but there are options offered under Settings that enable you to make Twitter truly your homepage away from home. From personalized backgrounds to password control, you can continue to make Twitter your own from here.

Changing Your Homepage Background

The Design tab offers a variety of prefabricated templates that include a background image and color scheme suited for it. You can customize templates to your own look with either a new background image (uploaded from your computer, similar to uploading avatars) by clicking on Change Background Image, or a new color scheme by clicking on Change Design

Colors. Changes are not live until you single-click the Save Changes button.

FIGURE 2.7   Custom backgrounds, provided they are kept to the basics, can give additional information about a user, but be wary about how they appear in a browser without sidebars (right) and with (left).

NOTE

Designing backgrounds like the one featured in Figure 2.7 is a clever way to give people additional information beyond the standard profile, but you should test the background in different screen resolutions and in browsers with sidebars collapsed and expanded. Otherwise you take a chance in having your additional information covered up by Twitter's interface.

Changing Your Password

If you have forgotten your password, you can, at the initial Sign In, have Twitter send you a reminder of what it was, provided you give them the email you opened the account with. The email is sent and you follow the steps through Twitter to set up a new password. You can also, once inside your account, create a new password by clicking Password tab found under Settings. These changes do not take effect until you single-click on Change and are given verification that the change has happened.

As with the other options found under Settings, Twitter also provides you with password tips on the right side of the page.

With Twitter now complete in its look and its profile, it is now time to reach out to people on the network, a worldwide group of users from various cultures and backgrounds that are probably sharing a lot in common with you.

Building the Network

With help from Twitter, you can start following people right away. Simply go to the top of your Twitter page and click on the Find People link. Twitter offers four options:

▶ **Find on Twitter**—This search option lets you look for people already on Twitter by username or their first and last name.

▶ **Find on Other Networks**—This option searches other networks such as Gmail and AOL for friends who have accounts registered with Twitter. After you log in, you can then follow them on Twitter.

▶ **Invite by Email**—Whether it is on a popular service like Yahoo!, Gmail, or AOL, or on a private server, you can email anyone in your address book and invite them onto Twitter.

▶ **Suggested Users**—Look familiar? This is the offered option at the beginning of your registration, now offering a bit more as you have a complete profile. Twitter takes a look at the details of your bio, finds active Twitter accounts, and then makes suggestions. With each one you check, Twitter lets you know whom you are following when you click on the Follow button.

Even with Twitter offering you assistance, it should not take long for people to find you. There are third-party websites such as Mr. Tweet (http://mrtweet.net) that assist Twitter users in building their respective networks. You can find out more about Mr. Tweet and building your network in Chapter 11, "Building and Rating Your Twitter Network." Instead of hopping ahead deep into the book, though, let's begin with someone that we can find easily on Twitter.

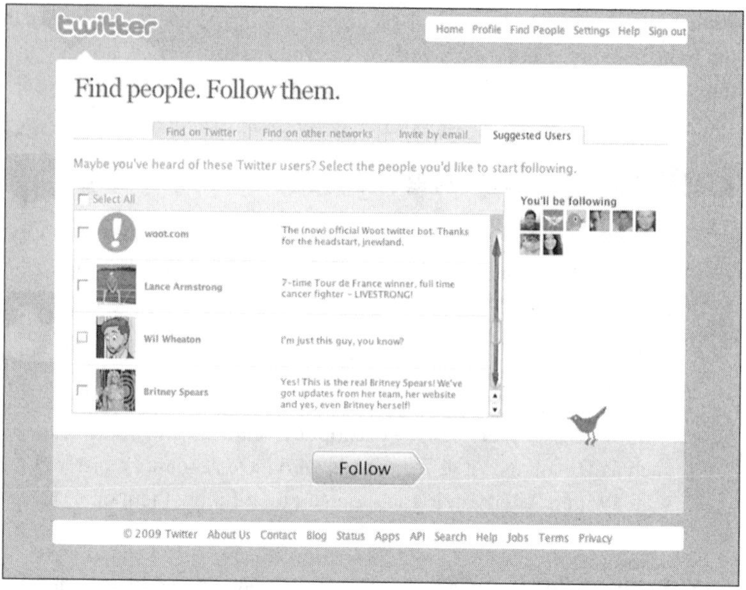

FIGURE 2.8   Now that you have Twitter the way you want it, it's time to build that network, and Twitter's Find People option is there to help.

Following Someone You Know on Twitter

Reaching out through Twitter to connect with others is not as intimidating as it sounds. Let's say you get a business card with a username on it. How do you find this person on Twitter? It's pretty simple, really.

1. With the person's username on hand, log into Twitter.

2. In the URL field of your browser, edit the address from http://twitter.com/home to http://twitter.com/username. (Examples: http://twitter.com/ITStudios, http://twitter.com/TeeMonster.)

3. After the user's Twitter page loads, single-click the Follow button under the user's avatar.

When people follow you, an email is sent that informs you *Someone Is Following You on Twitter* and then you are given the option to either visit their homepage and follow them or not. If the person following you strikes your interest, it is easy to return the gesture and follow them back on Twitter.

Following Someone That's Following You on Twitter

1. In your email notification, you see under Check Out User Name's Profile Here a URL for that user's Twitter homepage. Single-click the URL in the email or copy the URL.

2. Your browser should launch automatically if the URL is active in your email, or launch your browser of choice and paste the URL you copy from the email into the URL field. You find yourself at that user's Twitter homepage.

3. Review that Twitter's opening page. If you think this is a follower you want in your network, click on the Follow button under the user's avatar.

From here, you start tweeting. You start connecting. You let your network know what you are doing. That's all there is to it. From here, all you need to do is maintain your network, keep an eye on the activity, and participate in the chat or simply post your current status wherever you are, keeping those in your network informed.

Protecting Updates: The Good and the Bad

If you take a look under the Account tab of your Twitter settings, you see under Language the Protect My Updates option. As shown in Figure 2.9, your homepage looks a little different than the other Twitter pages that do not take advantage of this security feature. Protecting Updates keeps people outside of your network out of your feed entirely. You do not see what that person's feed is until you enter in a request and that request is granted. Once the request is approved, your feed is open to that person. Only your approved followers are granted access to your feed. This is just a way of protecting your feed from the general public, an added control over information coming to and from your Twitter account.

FIGURE 2.9 Twitter accounts with protected updates can offer you the option to send a request to the user for approval. When granted, the users' updates are revealed, but only to those in their Twitter network.

A positive in protecting your updates is that no one enters your network or even becomes privy to your activities or whereabouts unless you grant access. Protecting updates allows users to enjoy the social aspect of Twitter's network while providing extra security, if desired. The adverse effect to protecting updates is how this option works against Social Networking. Arriving to a page with protected updates can seem a touch defensive, especially with so many Twitter accounts free of such security measures.

Another deterrent for potential followers is that the protected updates limits them to only your name, bio, and any website you offer to serve as a reference to you. A lot can be found out about people based on their updates, but if these updates are protected, potential followers will either move on to other accounts or take a chance, watching you carefully as some phishers and spammers use this security measures to get their numbers up.

Consider, though, that security in Social Media is not always a bad thing. If you want to be careful, you can be. This is your choice, your call. While "open transparency" and sharing your mind is an appealing trait of Social Media, this does not mean that Twitter is an open invitation to check your brain at the door. There is nothing whatsoever wrong with being careful. It is your option. Just understand the option before implementing it.

Working with Protected Updates is a judgment call. There are pros and cons to having your updates protected, but remember where the option is located in your Settings. When you decide it is time to turn the measure on or off, you will know where this option is located.

Communicating with Others on Twitter

Your Twitter profile is completed, the avatar you have in place either promotes your professional brand or current state of mind, and you have made Twitter's complimentary homepage your own. Now comes the "hard sell" concerning this Social Networking tool: communicating with 140 characters or less.

There is a method to the madness of tweeting. Twitter makes you consider differently how to get your message across. Working with 140 characters is all about an economy of words, and in this lesson we focus on working with your inner editor.

Composing a "Tweet"

Twitter asks, "What are you doing?" Your reply is more commonly referred to as a *tweet*. Within the parameters of 140 characters, you might feel limited in what you can say, but you can say a lot with so little to work with.

Let's say your first tweet is

> I'm awake this morning and waiting for the coffee to brew. I've got a big day ahead of me with lots and lots of items on the To Do list. Yes, it looks a little overwhelming, but I'm feeling confident and ready to rock!

218 characters make up this tweet. That's too much. So let's break down what we want to convey.

The main points of this tweet are

- ▶ You're awake.
- ▶ The coffee is brewing.

▶ Your To Do list is very full for the day.

▶ You're feeling overwhelmed by it all.

▶ Your confidence level is high and you are feeling mighty!

You could space this single thought across two tweets, but some in your network might miss a tweet and will be confused by your incomplete thought.

I prefer tweets well under the 140-character limits. This allows people to retweet, drop in related links, and reference you without having to edit the original tweet too much. So, let's edit our original tweet to:

> Awake. Coffee brewing. Got a big day ahead with lots of "To Do" items, but I'm ready! RAR!

This update is now *under* 140 characters after these simple changes:

▶ Making "Awake" and "Coffee brewing" more active statements.

▶ "Lots and lots…" can easily be trimmed down to "lots…" and the intent is still clear.

▶ If you're feeling "ready," you can also insinuate the other sentiments.

▶ Although you eliminated some of the smaller subjects like "It's," the tweet still sounds as if you are having a conversation with someone. It's not choppy or disjointed.

All this, and I still have room for more. This, to me, is the *perfect* tweet: a statement with room to build on.

Exchanging URLs in Tweets

One way you can build on tweets is to make them interactive by including links to other websites. However, the 140-character limitation appears to make something so simple impossible, particularly if your link is something like this:

> http://www.amazon.com/Case-Pitchers-Pendant-Billibub-Baddings/ dp/1896944779?ie=UTF8&s=books&qid=1213066870&sr=1-1

This leaves you with only 27 characters remaining. If you want to do a book review on Twitter, it would have to be really short like *"Great read. Go buy now,"* which isn't much of a review (but a great endorsement, don't get me wrong!) because it doesn't even give a title or an author name to it. Wouldn't it be nice if we could shorten that massive URL to something like

http://is.gd/kuDQ

Then you could write a proper TwitReview around it like:

The Case of the Pitcher's Pendant is Tee Morris' latest Fantasy-Mystery novel. http://is.gd/kuDQ Just as good as the series' first book.

That's right. Both http://www.amazon.com/Case-Pitchers-Pendant-Billibub-Baddings/dp/1896944779?ie=UTF8&s=books&qid=1213066870&sr=1-1 and http://is.gd/kuDQ are the same link, but the latter is a shortened version of the original.

Condensing URLs Using Is.gd

Is.gd (found at http://is.gd) is one of many websites that takes long URLs and condenses them for Twitter clients, blogs, and other online services that allow for embedding URLs. These economized addresses work as aliases and reroute traffic to your website.

1. Find a URL (blogpost, webpage, et. al.) and then press either Command-A (Mac) or Control+A (PC) on your keyboard to select it. Press Command-C (Mac) or Control+C (PC) to copy the URL on to your clipboard.

2. Go to http://is.gd in your browser and paste (Command-V [Mac] or Control+V [PC]) into the empty data field the URL in its full form.

3. Single-click on the Compress That Address! button.

4. Is.gd takes you to a Results page with a new, condensed URL. Copy this URL and then use it in your tweet.

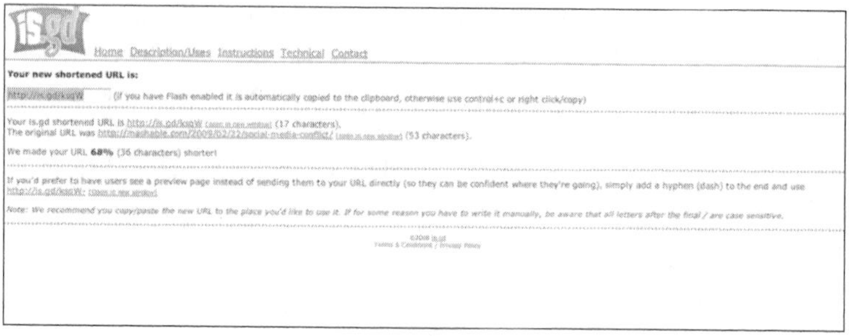

FIGURE 3.1 Is.gd takes long addresses for websites and prunes them down to a compact address suitable for Twitter.

Visiting Featured URLs

When a tweet appears with a link, either one you created or one you have received in your feed, you now have the ability to explore the Internet with your Twitter network as your guide.

1. Go to your Twitter homepage and find a tweet that features a link. It is usually a different color than the text, begins with http://, and will (hopefully) be shortened into a smaller size.

2. Single-click on the featured link.

3. Depending on your browser's Preferences, the link either opens in a new tab or a new window.

4. Close the tab or window to return to your Twitter homepage.

Is.gd is just one of many URL-shortening services you can find online. The others go by various names but accomplish the same results: a manageable URL for your 140-characters limit.

Posting Your Tweet

Now that you have your message composed (with a shortened URL for some variety), it is time to tweet it. For this next exercise, I'm going to give you something to tweet, a message well in the boundaries of Twitter's 140-character limit that includes a *hashtag* for tracking purposes. You find out more about hashtags in the next chapter.

1. Go to http://twitter.com/home on your Internet browser. If you are logged in and you told Twitter to remember you, you should still be logged in. (If not, go ahead and log back into Twitter.)

2. In the field under What Are You Doing? enter in the following:

   This is my first tweet. Thanks for the help on this, Tee Morris and Sams Publishing. #twitterin10

   At 97 characters in length, you should have plenty of space if you want to add in anything else like this page number, your current location, or even a quick "Hi, Mom!" Make sure that "#twitterin10" appears at the end of your tweet, as pictured in Figure 3.2.

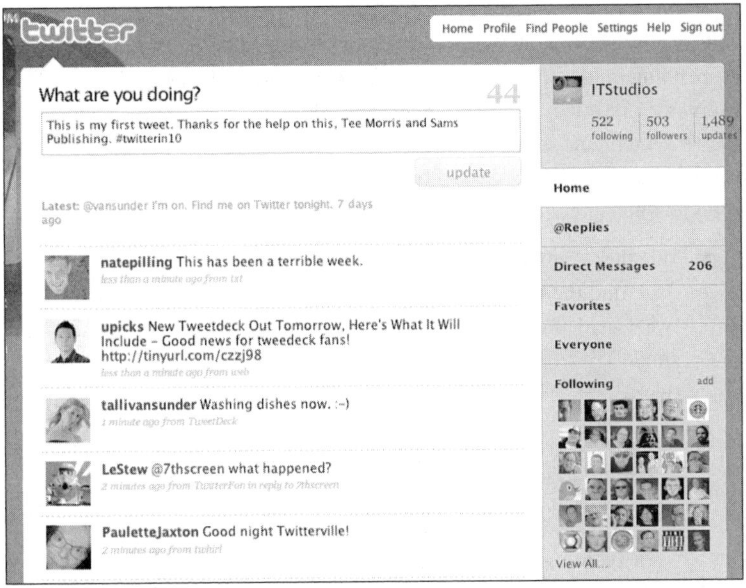

FIGURE 3.2 After your tweet is edited and ready to post, you are one click away from communicating with your community.

3. Single-click on the Update button. Your screen automatically refreshes and your message appears at the top of your visible timeline.

Your message is now sent across your network and in the Public Timeline to see. Type. Proof. Post. That's all there is to it!

Now that you are effectively tweeting, our next step is to see the response (if any) to your first tweet.

Replying to a Tweet

After you post your tweet, someone could ask in reply, "Who is Tee Morris and what does he have to do with Twitter?" This hypothetical tweet would appear in your timeline like this:

> TeeMonster @ITStudios Who is Tee Morris, and what does he have to do with Twitter?

This is a reply or an @Mention in Twitter. An @Mention begins with (depending on the interface you use) a user's avatar, the username, your username preceded by an "@" symbol, and finally the tweet. By adding in the @ symbol and username, the reply is "flagged" by Twitter as an active account and is then recognized by Twitter and third-party applications as a reply to you.

1. Whether you are in the @Mentions mode or your Timeline window, find the tweet you want to reply to. Either type into the tweet field @username or hover your mouse over the tweet and single-click on the arrow visible on the right side of the shaded tweet.

2. In the open tweet field, enter in a reply by clicking on the arrow, as seen in Figure 3.3. For the question from TeeMonster, the reply would look like this:

> @TeeMonster Tee Morris is the writer of *Teach Yourself Twitter in 10 Minutes*, available from Sams Publishing. #twitterin10

WARNING

Twitter usernames should be economical (defined here as anything under 10 characters) as the 140-character limitation does include the username.

FIGURE 3.3   Hovering your cursor over a tweet, the tweet is shaded and offers you the option to either Favorite it (the star icon) or reply to it (the arrow). Clicking the arrow adds the @Mention command automatically into your tweet field.

3. Single-click on the Reply button. Your screen automatically refreshes and the reply appears at the top of your visible time-line.

@Mentions provide you a quick connection to those following you, and you can give an @Mention to anyone on Twitter, even to people outside your network. Some third-party applications do not discriminate in how usernames are spelled, but others including Twitter.com do. Make sure, as seen in the example here, that you are case sensitive with the username, such as @TeeMonster and not @teemonster.

> **NOTE**
>
> In your homepage's interface, you can click on the arrow icon to reply to someone. If you want to reply to more than one person with a single tweet, simply click on the arrow of the person you want to include and the second @username appears. You can reply to as many people as you like. Just be wary of the character limitations.

There is another form of replying called the *Retweet*. How a retweet works is you single click the RT icon, or copy another Twitter's tweet, paste it into your own tweet field, and then precede the tweet with either **RETWEET:** or **RT:** to let people know you are passing the tweet along *your* network. If the retweet allows room for it, you can add in your own comments in parentheses. A retweet would look something like this:

> RT: **@YourUsername** @TeeMonster Tee Morris wrote *Teach Yourself Twitter in 10 Minutes* from Sams Publishing. (A great resource!) #twitterin10

Built-in Retweet functions are offered in third-party applications and serve as terrific methods in spreading a message, a link, or just something really cool throughout the Twitter network.

Replying to a Direct Message

When working in the website, you might miss receiving a *Direct Message* or a *DM* as it is referred to in the Twitterverse. @Mentions are visible in Twitter Searches, your own network's Timeline, or in your @Mentions Timeline. DMs are different. DMs are seen only by you and are not visible anywhere in Twitter other than in your account.

1. On your Twitter homepage, single-click on the Direct Messages option. This takes you to your account's Direct Messages page.

2. When you want to reply to a DM, you can hover your cursor over it. Similar to making @Mentions, the DM is shaded and offers two icons: an envelope (DM Reply) and a trash can (Delete DM). Single-click the Envelope icon, and you see in the Send drop-down menu that user's name.

NOTE

DMs can be sent from the main interface by typing in a lowercase "d" and a username. After you enter in the tweet field something like "d TeeMonster" or "d ITStudios" Twitter.com lets you know you are sending a DM to someone.

---

3. In the message field, type in your response.

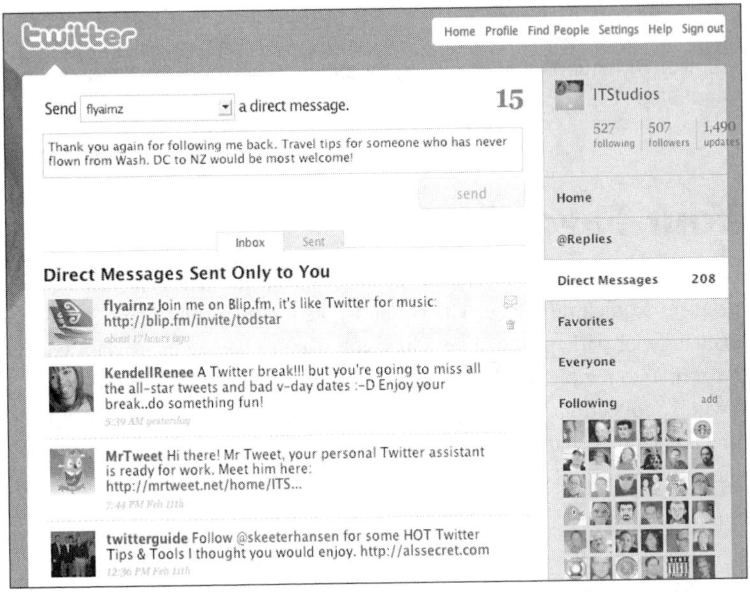

FIGURE 3.4 Hovering your cursor over a tweet offers you two options: Reply to a Direct Message and Delete a Direct Message. To reply to a DM, single-click the Envelope icon, type your message, and then click the Send button.

NOTE

Unlike @Mentions that can be sent to anyone on Twitter, DMs can be sent only to people following you and that you follow.

4. Single-click on the Send button. You will be rerouted to previous DMs you have sent with a confirmation that your message has been sent.

Although this is a private means of communication on Twitter, keep in mind that there will be a delay between DMs and no notification on your homepage that you have received a DM. (You can receive an email notification on a DM, however.) You can keep your Twitter discussions off the public network; but truly important conversations needing discretion and privacy are better held on Skype or some other chat application.

> **NOTE**
>
> Unlike @Mentions, you can reply to **only** one person with a Direct Message.

Your Favorites

On occasion, you might have an exchange on Twitter that you want or need for a quick reference. The tweet can be a particularly funny reply or exchange, or perhaps it can be a link you want to review later when you have time to read it. Whether you want to build your own "Best of Twitter" collection or bookmark for serious consideration, you want to make what is called a "Favorite." To make a tweet a Favorite, simply find the tweet on your Twitter.com page and single-click the star to the right of it.

The star icon, once clicked, saves tweets in a Favorites Bin located in your Twitter page and accessed there or through third-party clients. Twitter's Favorites feature tends to get overlooked as an option, but it can tell others a lot about you. Your Favorites, provided you are not protecting your updates, serve as an online scrapbook of favorite moments from a particular time.

So far we covered the basics of communicating and resource sharing on Twitter. In the upcoming chapters we work with various options that tap into its potential of media sharing, tracking trends and topics people are talking about, and how to work with Twitter away from Twitter.com.

Tracking Trends and Traffic on Twitter

Online, you will find sites designed to help you get the most out of Twitter and make your network a stronger one. Perhaps the best way of cultivating a strong network is staying connected with what is topical. The "whys" behind you being on Twitter, whether for fun or for the promise of profit, might vary; but it is always good to have an idea who is "paying attention" to you and what people are talking about. This is what keeps you in the know and gives others reasons to pay attention to your content. Covered here are the tools that assist you in tracking when you or your username are dropped in a conversation, when a topic of interest to you becomes a trend, and even give you an idea of how you are using Twitter. All of these things only help you increase your (positive) impact on the community you are building.

Tracking Trends on Twitter.com

In a recent upgrade, Twitter.com changed its homepage to include on the right side a Trending Topics section. Now you can see exactly what people are talking about across the entire network (not just your own) with this new option.

If you are looking for ways of finding people sharing like interests, accessing the Trending Topics offers you the ability to reach out and invite others to your network.

1. Go to your Twitter.com homepage and review the Trending Topics, located on the right side, below the Search field.

2. Find a topic of interest (one without a pound sign in front of it) and single-click it. In a new tab or window, Twitter produces search results for whatever topic you have accessed.

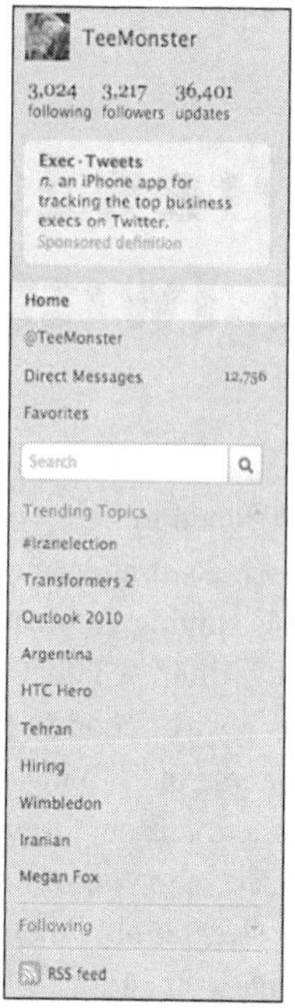

FIGURE 4.1 Through your homepage, trends—the topics that repeatedly appear across the Twitter network—are easily accessed.

WARNING

Keep in mind that this is a general search for whatever term you have accessed. This is not the same as tracking a topic with a user-created **hashtag**, explained later in this chapter. Open searches such as this (general terms, no # with it, etc.) can bring up both legitimate and bogus Twitter accounts.

---

3. From the search results, review various tweets commenting on your topic. When a tweet strikes your interest, click on the username and follow that person on Twitter.

> **NOTE**
>
> This open search across topics is a quick-and-simple way to find out what people are talking about, but depending on the topic you might need to sift through tweets that have nothing to do with what you are looking for. Regard clicking on a topic in the Trending Topics section as a generic term search on Google or some other search engine.

This approach to keep track of popular topics works in a pinch; but as mentioned in previous warnings, your successful results might vary. You also notice that some of the Trending Topics are marked with a pound sign (#). Those are topics of interest as well, set apart from generic searches because they are user-created (most of the time) and help narrow search parameters dramatically. These trending topics are also commonly referred to as *hashtags*.

Tracking Topics Using Hashtags

Hashtags are different from searching for generic terms on Twitter as they are user-created keywords specific to whatever topic you are tweeting or want to find out more about. They have been criticized for using up valuable characters from Twitter's 140-character limit and for being trivialized in casual conversations. When it comes to raising awareness or visibility on Twitter, however, hashtags have proven time and again to be the most effective way of doing so.

Hashtags are free. There is no real setup involved. They are easy to incorporate and even easier to use.

1. In Twitter or on your preferred Twitter client, compose the following tweet:

   Right now, I am learning how to use hashtags. Thank you, Tee Morris for teaching this.

   Do not send this tweet just yet.

2. At the end of this tweet, add #twitterin10 and then send your tweet.

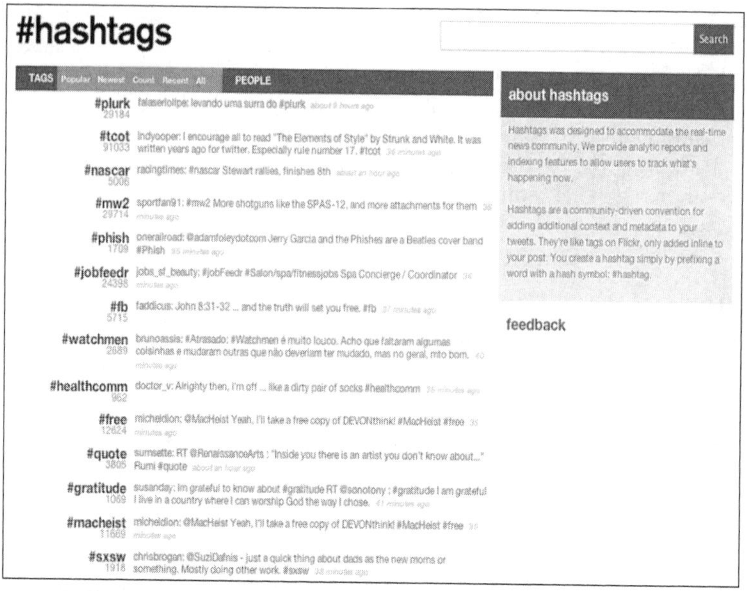

FIGURE 4.2   Track trends that you start or raise awareness of a cause with hashtags.

3. To track who else is using the hashtag you have just incorporated, go to http://hashtags.org and perform a search in the Search field, located in the upper-right section of the website.

> **WARNING**
>
> Spammers have been attempting to work around the user-generated originality of hashtags by entering into automated Twitter services a hashtag and generating it into their tweets. Although hashtags, on a whole, are still easy to narrow searches and ensure you are networking with real people, be aware that some are trying to find loopholes.

4. Return to your Twitter homepage; and under Trending Topics, click on a trend that is a hashtag (marked with a pound sign). The tweets appearing in your results feature tweets carrying that hashtag.

Incorporating hashtags, as seen here, isn't the hard part. The hard part is remembering to add the hashtag at the end of your tweet, and remain consistent in what you use for your hashtag. For example, the following hashtags are considered the same topic by Twitter:

- ▶ #twitterin10

- ▶ #TwitterIn10

- ▶ #TWITTERIN10

These hashtags, however, will not offer the same search results:

- ▶ #twitterinten

- ▶ #Twitter_in_10

- ▶ #TWITTER-IN-10

Rules of thumb when it comes to hashtags are simple:

- ▶ Use a quick, easy-to-recall keyword for your hashtag. Keep it compact.

- ▶ Publicize what the keyword is. Use it when you can to let people know what you want to use. Use it in print ads, presentations, blogs, and so on.

- ▶ Remember to be consistent with it, and make sure others are consistent with it.

- ▶ Remember to add it to the end of your tweets.

NOTE

TweetDeck will, when you reply to a tweet that has a hashtag in it, automatically add in hashtags at the end of your reply.

Hashtags, along with the other tools mentioned here, provide ways to increase your community, improve your networking skills, and raise awareness for your causes and movements. This is all part of the potential found in Social Networking.

Trending Topics and hashtags all help you increase your visibility on Twitter. These, and other services Twitter recognizes, stem from the most basic of tracking methods: the search engine. *Twitter Search* is one of the more popular engines that offer users the ability to search across the network for trends, people, or other topics featured in tweets. Twitter Search has proven to be so reliable that it appears in many third-party clients. It's easy to use and a tool worth employing.

Using Twitter Search

With Google-esque efficiency, Twitter Search (http://search.twitter.com) can search throughout all Public Timeline tweets the keywords, names, and places you enter into the Twitter Search field. As with hashtags and Trending Topics, Twitter Search is a snap to use.

FIGURE 4.3   Twitter Search is the Google of Twitter, giving you the ability to search terms, usernames, and people mentioned in feeds across the network.

1. Go to http://search/twitter.com and type into the empty data field a term, trend, or keyword (including a hashtag) you want to search for in the network. Single-click on the Search button.

This might seem like all there is to Twitter Search, but there is a feature of Twitter Search worth mentioning here....

2. In the top-right corner of the search results, you see an RSS logo followed by a Feed for This Query link. Single-clicking that automatically takes you to your default RSS reader, allowing you to subscribe to this query as a feed. Whenever new instances of this query appear in Twitter, you are notified in your RSS reader.

> **NOTE**
>
> By subscribing to a Twitter Search, you can receive via RSS the Twitter-version of a Google Alert to find out who is tweeting what about you or topics of interest to you. Twitter Search is another way you can grow your network: searching on terms of like interest, subscribing to them with an RSS reader, and then reviewing users who tweet about them. You can also contact them at random, formally introducing yourself to them.

Twitter Search is regarded so highly as a Twitter essential that many third-party clients have built Twitter Search directly into their interfaces, as shown in Chapters 6, "Using Third-Party Applications: Twhirl," and 7, "Using Third-Party Applications: TweetDeck." With Twitter Search so readily accessible, you can easily explore Twitter and discover its influence not only on your network, but also on your overall habits on the network.

Tracking Your Twitter Habits with TweetStats

Now that you're tracking the topics that are hot on Twitter, how about tracking your own personal trends. How do you use Twitter? Who do you talk to? When are you online? Many services are coming online that take a look at your own habits, but one of the original evaluators out there that continues to keep an unbiased look at how you use Twitter is TweetStats (http://tweetstats.com). TweetStats takes a look at your account and breaks down your usage into a variety of categories that tell you who you talk to, when you're online, what your peak hours are, and also what you talk about. It's a quick glance of what kind of Twitter user you are.

1. Go to http://tweetstats.com and enter your Twitter username.

2. Single-click the Graph My Tweets! button. TweetStats reviews your overall history and, after a few moments, presents a breakdown of your Twitter habits. The results appear something similar to Figure 4.4.

> **WARNING**
>
> If your updates are protected, TweetStats cannot evaluate your account usage. This is the trade-off for not asking for passwords. If you want to be assessed, your timeline must be **public**, not **protected**.

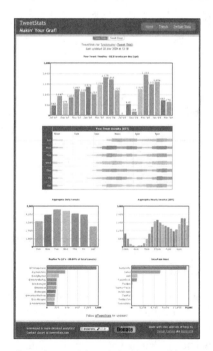

FIGURE 4.4 TweetStats is a quick-and-simple graphic representation of when you tweet, what you use to tweet with, and even what your popular tweet topics are.

3. After reviewing your data, single-click on the Tweet Cloud tab to view your most commonly tweeted terms.

4. If you want to send any of these results as a tweet, single-click on the Tweet This! link at the top of each result page. You are then rerouted to your Twitter homepage with a tweet all set and ready to send.

The information TweetStats generates is hardly private information; therefore, no password is required to review any active Twitter account. All you need to do is enter in a username and review the results. You can use TweetStats to review your account activity whereas others can use it to try to find the best time to find you online.

The various graphs you find at TweetStats cover

▶ **Tweet Timeline**—A monthly bar graph shows the progression of your tweeting habits, from humble beginnings to whatever level your account reaches. TweetStats also calculates your average tweets per day.

▶ **Tweet Density**—The breakdown of when you are on Twitter, on a daily and weekly basis. Darker, thicker portions of the graph are the times your tweets are most frequent.

▶ **Daily and Hourly Tweets**—TweetStats looks at time stamps of your Twitter stream and reports days and hours in which you tweet the most and the least.

▶ **Replies To**—This graph shows the ten users you reply to the most. For people wanting to develop a network, this is a handy tool to review potential additions.

▶ **Interface Used**—A breakdown of which available third-party Twitter clients are used. This is a terrific statistic if you are considering or wanting to test spin Twitter applications.

TweetStats, along with assessing individual statistics, offers Trends and Twitter Stats just as your Twitter homepage does.

> **NOTE**
>
> Twitalyzer (http://www.twitalyzer.com/, pictured in Figure 4.5) is similar to TweetStats in that it evaluates the details of your Twitter account. However, Twitalyzer goes deeper into what kind of Twitter user you are. Along with Usage (or what they call **Velocity**), you are given an evaluation on your **Influence, Signal-to-Noise Ratio, Generosity,** and **Clout.** Twitalyzer is a terrific detailed breakdown of your Twitter behavior, but it's real power coming out after return visits that assesses your growth over time. Twitalyzer's comparison tools, against you and other users, give you goals and benchmarks on what to gauge growth and development. It's a terrific service to use in developing your Twitter presence.

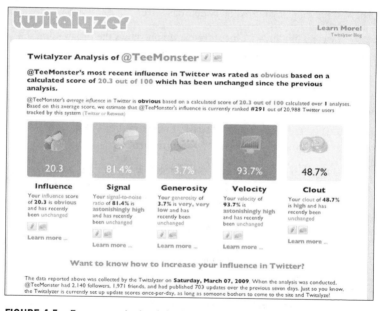

FIGURE 4.5   For a more in-depth look at how you interact with your network, many Twitter users turn to Twitalyzer.

Tracking your own activity on Twitter is just as essential as tracking the overall trends the network follows. Such self-evaluation makes you a better user and also assists you in creating a better network. How? By monitoring your own traffic, you find out what you talk about and to whom you directly reply or mention. You also can gauge your usage. Are you frequent during the day, at night, or is your frequency harder to pin down? In your tweet cloud, the evidence is most telling—what do you talk about *most frequently?* Based on this, you can find out just how engaging you are as a Twitter user.

WARNING

Although I endorse Twitalyzer, make sure you do not confuse it with TwitterAnalyzer. TwitterAnalyzer claims to offer the same services, but I hold its security in question as TwitterAnalyzer promotes itself via spamming techniques under bogus user accounts.

Another way to track your impact, and the overall reaction and participation of your networks, is by tracking traffic following links you feature in your Twitter feed. Is.gd, featured in Chapter 3, "Communicating with Others on Twitter," merely shortens your URLs; but *Bit.ly* goes one step further and gives you the economy in your URL character count while offering the power of TweetStats.

Tracking Your Traffic Using Bit.ly

The URL-condensing website Bit.ly (http://bit.ly) offers a little more than other URL-condensing services. Bit.ly is like Is.gd because it shortens websites, but Bit.ly goes a bit further than Is.gd in that it maintains a database for you and can also track traffic visiting your shared websites when live on Twitter.

Due to Bit.ly's extra features, you need to set up an account. This might seem unsettling for users worried about privacy and access issues, but Bit.ly is secure. It's also a free account and enables you to access the higher features.

1. Find a long URL (blogpost, webpage, and such), single-click the URL in your browser, and press either Command-A (Mac) or Control+A (PC) on your keyboard.

2. Press Command-C (Mac) or Control+C (PC) to copy the URL on to your clipboard.

3. Go to http://bit.ly in your browser and paste the URL (Command-V [Mac] or Control+V [PC]) into the empty data field in its full, unaltered form. If you want to create a custom URL for this link, you can do so here.

4. Single-click on the Shorten button.

5. After your URL is shortened, click the Copy link to get the link on your clipboard.

6. Go to your browser and paste into the URL field your Bit.ly URL; then add a plus sign at the end of it. (For example, you copied http://bit.ly/TeeOnFB, but in your browser enter http://bit.ly/TeeOnFB+.)

7. Press Return or Enter on your keyboard to view statistics on traffic you're generating.

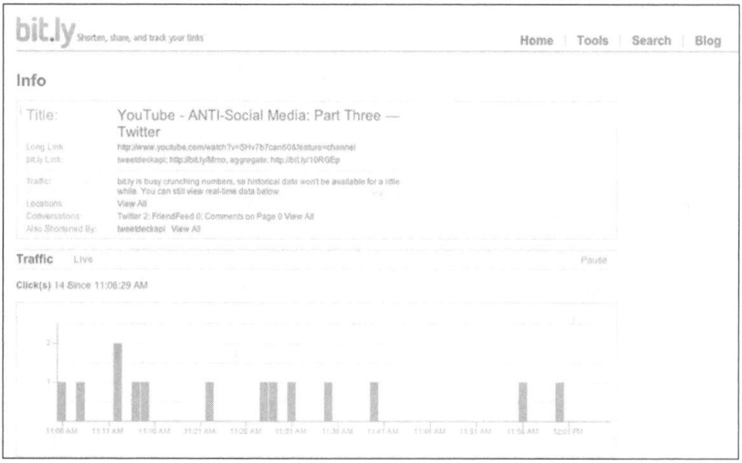

FIGURE 4.6   Bit.ly tracks statistics of the traffic you generate through the links you tweet, including origins of the traffic, retweets of the links, and any additional metadata associated with the original link.

Bit.ly, as shown in Figure 4.6, creates a bar graph that progresses in real time across your screen with traffic. Statistics also include a breakdown of where your hits are coming from in the world. This tracking option, from a marketing and public relations perspective, gives you a terrific assessment of the online activity your Twitter presence generates. Finally, Bit.ly maintains a running tally of shortened URLs you have created, easily accessed and circulated through your feed.

This chapter has given you a good focus on tracking and assessing your effectiveness on Twitter. Now with tracking awareness, themes, and trends on Twitter, we move into offering more to your network in the ways of shared media. Twitter began humbly enough with an exchange of links; but now with the development of various sites such as 12seconds.tv, TwitPic, and MobyPicture, aural and visual resources are only a tweet away.

Incorporating Media with Twitter

With Twitter's popularity, developers arrived that wanted more from Twitter. These creative minds put together websites offering to take users out of their textual world and bring them into a more visual one. This began a new trend with tweeting: making the most of 140 characters with the help of images, audio, and video.

TwitPic

In various third-party clients covered in later chapters, you might see the icon of a camera, button, or link labeled TwitPic. *TwitPic* (http://twitpic.com) is Flickr (http://flickr.com) for Twitter, a photographer's haven where photos from your hard drive or directly from your mobile phone can be uploaded and shared with your network. Far from the many options Flickr offers, TwitPic does enable you to easily distribute photos with your Twitter network in only a few steps.

One of TwitPic's best features is that your TwitPic account is already set up. Simply go to http://twitpic.com and log in with your Twitter username and password. (Yes, TwitPic is a safe site to share your password with.) Clicking on the Home link at the top of TwitPic's Welcome page takes you to your TwitPic homepage, as seen in Figure 5.1.

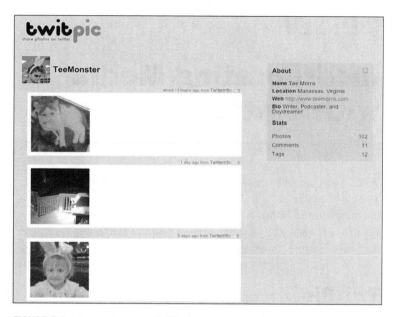

FIGURE 5.1 Accessing your TwitPic homepage requires the same login as your Twitter account.

Uploading Pictures on TwitPic

Unlike what you see in Figure 5.1 (http://twitpic.com/photos/TeeMonster), you probably do not have any pictures uploaded. Yet. So, wherever you have pictures suitable for sharing with your network accessible on your computer, let's get some content uploaded to your TwitPic account.

1. Go to http://twitpic.com and log in with your Twitter account settings. After you log in, single-click on the Upload Photo link at the top of the page to go to the Upload and Post a Photo interface.

2. Click on the Browse button to browse your computer for a photograph. When you find a photo you want to share on your Twitter network, click OK to return to TwitPic.

3. In the next field, enter in any information (funny caption, location, or subject I.D.) for the photo and then click the Upload button.

The photo is uploaded onto your TwitPic (and in its original size, TwitPic resizes it for preview purposes in the same way Flickr does) homepage. In a few moments, a tweet featuring a TwitPic URL and your caption appears in your Public Timeline. If the picture is a vertical shot and uploads horizontally, viewers can rotate it to an upright position. After uploading if you decide that you would rather not have the photo displayed, simply click on your Twitter Username in the right portion of the browser window. That takes you to your collection of photos, similar to what is shown in Figure 5.1. When there, single-click the Delete (trash can) icon grouped with the photo you want to delete.

> **WARNING**
>
> You can use TwitPic to send images with DMs, but remember that only the DMs accompanying them are kept private. The image itself is made public. This means any image of a sensitive, squeamish, or saucy nature will be present in a **public** TwitPic stream.
>
> Also, some third-party clients will simply make a DM public if a TwitPic link is detected. Best to keep this in mind when working with images on Twitter.

TwitPic.com makes it just that easy to share photos across your network. In later chapters concerning desktop and mobile clients, TwitPic integration is covered in detail, and the end of this chapter features *Power Twitter's* built-in function for your Twitter.com homepage. With the capability of mobile phones taking more and more print-worthy photographs, working with TwitPic is essential, particularly when the situation just cannot be accurately described in 140 characters.

TwitPic was one of the original online utilities that offered Twitter users the option to add media into your Twitter stream. Following in its footsteps are other services such as Twitgoo and TweetPhoto for starters. A handful of these photo sharing sites are extending their extrasensory reach, though, and offering a few extra features for their users.

Mobypicture

Entrepreneur Mathys van Abbe went online with Mobypicture (http://www.mobypicture.com) in June 2008, and from the Netherlands this online utility grew to offer its users not only the ability to exchange photos, but also audio and video across their networks. The site enables users to share a wide array of media across many social networks. Along with Twitter, Mobypicture also offers support for other networks like Flickr, Facebook, YouTube, Wordpress-powered blogs, and others.

FIGURE 5.2   Mobypicture enables you to share photos, audio, and video with your Twitter network, and with other Social Networking platforms.

Uploading Pictures on Mobypicture

Setting up an account with Mobypicture is also a snap because you can use your Twitter account credentials and sign in immediately. Once logged in, uploading can begin.

1. Go to http://mobypicture.com and log in with your Twitter account by single-clicking on the login link at the top of the page. (When logged in, you see your username in place of the Login and Sign up links.)

> **WARNING**
>
> Some third-party Twitter utilities ask for username and passwords. Depending on what the utility offers, consider if you actually want to do this. Passwords should not be surrendered lightly. As other Twitter clients offer support for TwitPic and Mobypicture, these sites are considered safe territory. Make certain you give your login credentials for something worthwhile and productive.

2. Single-click on the Upload link at the top of the page to go to the Upload Media interface.

3. Click on the Select button to browse your computer for a photograph. When you find a photo you want to share on your Twitter network, click OK to return to Mobypicture.

4. Give the picture a title, quick description, and location of where it was taken and any relevant tags (keywords useful in searching for a photograph) for this photo.

5. Single-click the Upload button and a progress bar appears, uploading the image.

6. When uploading is completed, the image can be seen by scrolling down to the menu labeled You. Click the Startpage link and then click the My Stream tab. There, you see a thumbnail of your image.

Similar to Flickr, Mobypicture uploads your photo in its original size, resizes it for preview purposes, and then—on single-clicking it—offers you a variety of sizes for download. Uploading for video and audio are identical; but if the file does not meet the standards Mobypicture requests from its users, the file will not be entered into the interface.

> **WARNING**
>
> In writing *Sams Teach Yourself Twitter in 10 Minutes*, nowhere on the site or in the blog could be found desired video formats or preferred compression. Three attempts were made to upload video compressed at YouTube standards and none worked. Attempts with lower-quality video were successful; so if you use Mobypicture for video, prepare for trial and error.

Mobypicture is a one-stop shop for your audio and video needs, but when it comes to the Internet, options are always a good thing to have. If you are looking for an alternative to the Swiss Army knife of media, that is Mobypicture; you can turn to other online utilities to bring media to your Twitter networks.

Using YouTube with Twitter

Easily the most popular video-sharing service online with millions upon millions of video clips online and ready for viewing, *YouTube* (http://youtube.com) has made sharing video online an easy and painless process. If you have never used the service before, YouTube opens its servers to people around the world to upload videos and share them with the world through the main YouTube.com site or through blog distribution.

FIGURE 5.3   YouTube now offers channel hosts the ability to let people know when new content goes live.

Now, YouTube offers Twitter integration, making notification of new content going live even easier.

1. If you have a YouTube account, log into YouTube.

2. Roll your cursor over the Upload button located in the upper-right corner of YouTube's interface and select Upload Video File from your options. Single-click the Upload Video button.

3. From the Select File window, browse your computer and find a video file for you to upload on to YouTube. Select the video file and then single-click on Select to advance to the details page.

NOTE

When preparing video for YouTube, make sure you adhere to its video compression standards:

▶ Size: 2GB

▶ Playback length: 10 minutes

▶ Resolution: 1280 x 720 (16x9 HD) or 640 x 480 (4:3 SD)

▶ Codec: H.264, MPEG-2 or MPEG-4 preferred

▶ Audio: MP3 or AAC, 44.1kHz, Stereo

---

4. While you have the progress bar showing the uploading process, fill in details on the clip which will display on the video's page. Click on the Save Changes button to accept these details.

5. Below the option to upload an additional video, you see Autoshare Options. In the Add Services section, single-click the Twitter option.

NOTE

Confirm that you are logged into your Twitter account on your browser. These next steps authenticate YouTube to whichever Twitter account you are logged into in your browser.

---

6. You might be prompted in a new window to enter in your Gmail/Google/YouTube password for authentication. Do so. Twitter then asks if you want to Allow or Deny Google access. Click the Allow button.

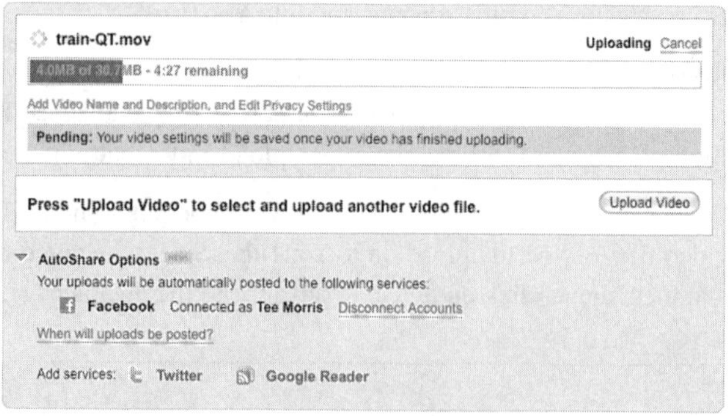

FIGURE 5.4   With its latest option, AutoShare, YouTube now integrates directly with Twitter in letting people know you have new video online.

7. In YouTube your Twitter account appears in the AutoShare Options. When your YouTube video is live on your channel, your network is notified with a simple post reading:

I uploaded a YouTube video – (title of the video) (truncated URL)

NOTE

The YouTube-generated tweet will not happen automatically. Video, when uploaded to YouTube, must also be processed by the YouTube servers for optimum playback. Depending on the running length and resolution of the video, this might take some time.

YouTube and Twitter now work together as yet another notification system to let people worldwide know when you have uploaded new content. Your videos link is distributed automatically across your network and then becomes viral if your network passes it along through a series of retweets.

This latest innovation from YouTube opens an entirely new way to distribute video via truncated URLs in tweets. It is a fantastic option to explore and makes YouTube and Twitter more powerful tools in Social Networking. But how would Twitter and YouTube *together* work? A true combination of video sharing combined with the limitations of Twitter. Could something like that work?

Actually, it already is, and this service is making strides to integrate fully with Twitter.

Video + Twitter = 12seconds.tv

People tend to be the most skeptical concerning Twitter on finding out they can state their mind in only 140 characters or less. Imagine those same skeptics if they are told of a service that enables you to record your video messages and instantly share them, but you're allowed only 12 seconds for recording purposes.

Twelve seconds?! Why only 12 seconds?

"Because anything longer is boring," state the creators of 12seconds.tv (http://12seconds.tv). "Exactly 12 seconds of video is the ideal amount of time to keep anything interesting."

1. Go to http://12seconds.tv and click on the Sign in/Register link in the top-right portion of your browser. You will be prompted to work with either your Facebook account or your Twitter account, or you have an option to create a brand new account. Single-click the Twitter option in the prompt window.

2. Similar to YouTube, Twitter asks if you want to Allow or Deny 12seconds access. Click the Allow button.

> **NOTE**
>
> As mentioned in the previous YouTube exercise, confirm that you are logged into your Twitter account on your browser. Step 2 authenticates whichever Twitter account you are currently logged into in your browser.

3. After you log into your 12seconds.tv account, single-click on the Record icon in the Make a 12 row of options. As shown in Figure 5.5, you will be prompted to confirm and test your web camera settings. When everything works fine and you see yourself in the Preview window, click Close.

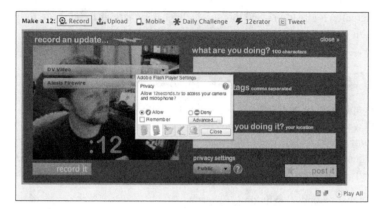

FIGURE 5.5   The Twitter for television, 12seconds.tv, taps into your web camera's preferences to get you all set and ready to record your thoughts.

NOTE

Make sure your browser runs the latest Adobe Flash player. You might be prompted to make an upgrade, or you can simply pay a visit to http://get.adobe.com/flashplayer/ for the latest plug-ins.

---

4. Fill in the descriptive tags for your video and then press the Record It button. You then see on the screen a countdown clock telling you exactly how many seconds you have remaining.

5. After recording, you can either single-click the Cancel & Re-record link to record your message again, single-click the Post It button to make your video live, or single-click the Close option in the top-right corner of the interface to delete the recording completely.

Your message is now live and shared instantly with your network; the tweet given a truncated URL leading your network back to 12seconds.tv.

> **NOTE**
>
> Along with the network you build on Twitter, you can also build a second network of people both affiliated with and independent of Twitter on 12seconds.tv. In the Search bar provided, you can search for other Twitter users and follow them here. You can also reach out to people not on Twitter by reviewing other videos featured under the Featured, Popular, or Everyone links, clicking on their usernames, and following them. With the growth of your 12seconds network, you will notice more activity in some desktop clients such as TweetDeck, covered in Chapter 7, "Using Third-Party Applications: TweetDeck," of this book.

12seconds.tv truly is the video version of Twitter, giving you the ability to send out quick video updates to your network using your computer's web cam or mobile phone. You speak off-the-cuff or rehearse a quick, focused message. You do what you need to do and then you're done.

Now we bring all these elements—links, photos, and various media—together at the place where we started: Twitter.com.

Power Twitter for Firefox

So far, in working with media, we have been circulating links that take people to other websites; but as it goes with links exchanged between users, some less-than-ethical professionals tend to use services such as Twitter to drive traffic to their own sites or online media whether people want to go there or not. This practice has become so common that Bit.ly (covered in Chapter 4, "Tracking Trends and Traffic on Twitter") has now, as reported by TechCrunch on July 16, 2009 (http://ow.ly/htRH), begun warning people who click on these links that the content on the other end of the link might contain unsolicited content.

For Twitter users getting from site to site with Firefox (http://mozilla.com), there is a solution for previewing links without ever leaving your Twitter.com homepage. This solution also enables you to preview images shared within your network and even play audio and video directly through your homepage. This solution is one of many *add-ons* (user-developed extensions) that Mozilla's site offers for Firefox, and not only changes how you review and preview your network's shared media, but also how you interface with Twitter all together. This solution is *Power Twitter* (http://bit.ly/PowerTwitterAddOn).

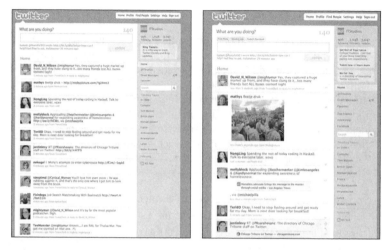

FIGURE 5.6 Power Twitter takes your Twitter homepage (left, without Power Twitter) and adds a variety of functions and features (right, with Power Twitter) that help with managing and previewing shared media.

Installing Power Twitter

As you see in the right side of Figure 5.6, Power Twitter enhances the UI of your Twitter.com homepage with a variety of options. Installation of Power Twitter into Firefox (if you have never installed an add-on onto your browser) is a breeze.

1. Go to http://bit.ly/PowerTwitterAddOn and single-click the green Add to Firefox button.

2. Your Firefox browser prompts you to install the Add-On. Click Install Now and then when the installation is complete, click the Restart Firefox button at the top-right portion of the Add-Ons window.

3. After Firefox relaunches, go to your Twitter homepage. (If you didn't have it open already—Forefox restores your previous session on relaunch.)

4. If you see Power added to the Twitter logo and your UI and Twitter stream appear as the right image of Figure 5.6, you are now running Power Twitter. If not, go to Tools > Add-Ons in Firefox to see if the extension is installed and running.

NOTE

If that was your first Firefox Add-On installation, congratulations! It's just that easy to extend the capabilities of your browser. When you can, explore Mozilla's website for other terrific add-ons for Twitter and many other Social Networking sites. Type Social Networking into the Firefox Search Query and leave the menu set on the All Add-Ons option. Single-click the green arrow to browse the results to see what is available.

The Power Twitter Experience

With Power Twitter running, let's take a look at how it changes our Twitter homepage's UI and incorporating media into our feed.

1. With Power Twitter activated, compose a tweet with a URL. If you don't have one in mind, feel free to use this one:

   I am now officially a Power Twitter, thanks to the help of Tee Morris and http://bit.ly/twitterin10 #twitterin10

2. Single-click Update and your tweet appears at the top of the feed. After one second or two, your Bit.ly (or whichever URL shortener you use) link will be swapped out for a brief description of what your link is directed to.

3. Next, open a new window or tab and find a long URL that is in need of trimming. Copy the URL and then return to your Twitter homepage.

4. Single-click the Shorten Link option just above the tweet field. You will be prompted to paste the link into a field. Do so, and single-click the Shorten button.

WARNING

When you want to shorten a URL, make sure you do not compose your tweet before attempting to shorten a URL. Any text in the Compose field is erased when you use Power Twitter to shorten a URL. (And note—Power Twitter warns you of this, too!)

5. You return to your homepage with a Bit.ly URL in the tweet field. Compose your tweet around the condensed link and click Update to send it out to your network.

6. Single-click on the Post Photo option and then click the Choose File button to find a photograph on your computer you would like to share with your network.

FIGURE 5.7 When you use Power Twitter's Post Photo option, the image is uploaded to TwitPic (top) and then displayed in your feed (bottom) after sending.

7. When the image upload is complete, you see a thumbnail of the image to the right of the tweet field and a TwitPic URL for it. Compose a tweet with it and click Update to send it out to your network.

NOTE

While you see brief descriptions of links, previews of images, and playback UIs for media, anyone not using Power Twitter will see condensed URLs.

8. When the image upload is complete, you see a thumbnail of the image to the right of the tweet field and a TwitPic URL for it. Compose a tweet with it and click Update to send it out to your network.

9. To best illustrate video or audio through Power Twitter, you need to return to YouTube and single-click the yellow Upload button. Find either a small video (no more than 10 seconds) to upload, and begin the uploading procedure.

NOTE

You can also use your webcam and produce quick-and simple videos for YouTube. The interface that gets YouTube to recognize your webcam is identical to the setup previously seen in this chapter in step 3 and Figure 5.5 of Twitter + Video = 12seconds.tv.

10. When the image has uploaded *and been processed* (something that, as previously mentioned, can take a while, depending on the video uploaded) by YouTube, a tweet is generated and appears in a Power Twitter homepage as an embedded YouTube clip.

NOTE

Video generated by 12seconds.tv does not appear as embedded clips in your Power Twitter feed. It appears as a link leading back to your 12seconds account.

For a full list of features and what Power Twitter brings to your Twitter homepage's UI, visit the developers' website at http://bit.ly/ptfeatures for a complete breakdown of what is offered in the current version.

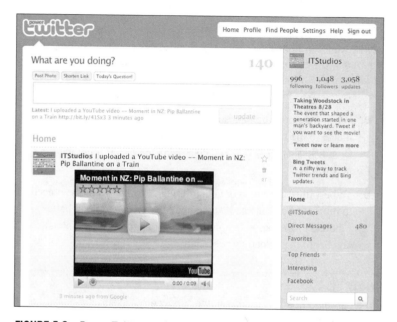

FIGURE 5.8   Power Twitter renders video and audio links as embedded video in tweets.

The various tools we covered here have been geared for incorporating media into your Twitter feed to broaden the impact of your message by incorporating images, audio, and video. You now have ways to bringing your network even closer to the action, adding a visual aspect to your tweets. Tweets now "speak 1,000 words" with the integration of TwitPic, and with 12seconds you can combine the spontaneity of tweets with the impact of video. All these elements then come together with the incorporation of Power Twitter. The utilities I feature in *Sams Teach Yourself Twitter in 10 Minutes* are only a few of many similar services that are online, and no doubt there will be more sites coming that will continue to help you make the most of your 140 characters. With this chapter and the resources listed at the end of this title, you are sure to find new and seemingly custom-designed services to help you syndicate and incorporate varying forms of media in your Twitter stream.

LESSON 6

Using Third-Party Applications: Twhirl

Third-party desktop applications are utilities that take Twitter into a higher level of efficiency by fetching your tweets and displaying them as they come in. *Twhirl* (http://www.twhirl.org) first appeared in the Twitterverse at the beginning of 2008 and quickly became a popular third-party desktop application. Twhirl tends to work best with accounts that are new or that have followers numbering in the hundreds, offering an expanded integration with other online services such as TwitPic, FriendFeed, Ping.fm and Seesmic. It's no surprise, considering Twhirl's intuitive approach to Twitter, that this client is considered one of the best available.

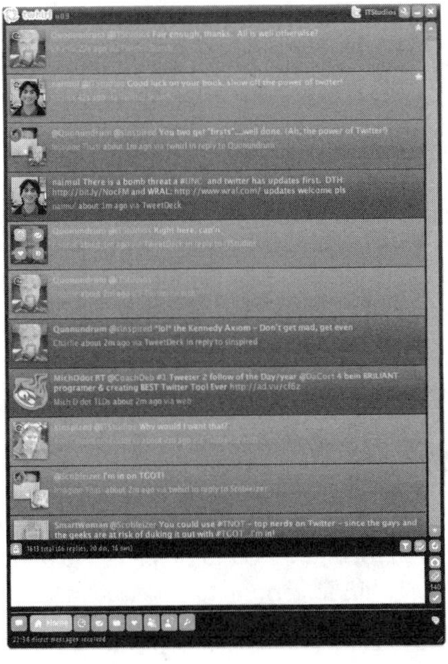

FIGURE 6.1 Twhirl, one of the most popular Twitter clients in use, provides users with a compact interface and expanded capabilities.

Downloading and Installing Twhirl

Twhirl has an extra step involved before installation and setup. You need to have *Adobe AIR* installed on your computer. Without AIR, Twhirl can't run. Fortunately, Adobe AIR is free to download at http://get.adobe.com/air.

NOTE

Adobe AIR brings Internet content to you in real time without the confines of a browser. AIR utilizes current online resources for developers to create custom applications that run on popular operating systems such as Mac and Windows.

What is imperative to know about this download is that it is free, safe, and has the support of Adobe behind it.

---

1. Download a copy of Adobe AIR from Adobe Systems. You can follow the link from the Twhirl home page to the download location on Adobe's website.

2. Install Adobe AIR on your computer. After installation is verified, return to Twhirl's homepage and download the latest version.

3. Install Twhirl and follow the login procedures for your Twitter account by entering in your username and password.

4. When you initially log in, there is a lot of activity. Tabs pop up, chimes might go off, and your Twhirl window fills with tweets. All this is normal. When Twhirl is up and running, you can configure it.

Configuring Twhirl

The client is up and running, but it might not be running the way we would prefer it to run. Before we get to tweeting and retrieving tweets from it, let's set up Twhirl to perform to our standards.

1. At the top-right corner of Twhirl's window, you should see a wrench icon. Single-click on the wrench to access Configuration.

2. Under the General options, you can set up Twhirl to

▶ Open This (Current) Account When Twhirl Launches

▶ Keep Twhirl Visible at All Times (labeled "Always on Top")

▶ Hide Twhirl When Minimized

▶ Spell-Check Tweets During Composition

▶ Access Twitter Profiles Either Directly in Twhirl or Via Users' Home Page

▶ Format Retweets in a Custom Fashion

▶ Use tweets from Twhirl to Update Status in Other Social Networks

Set up Twhirl to your desired specifications and then move on to the Visual tab.

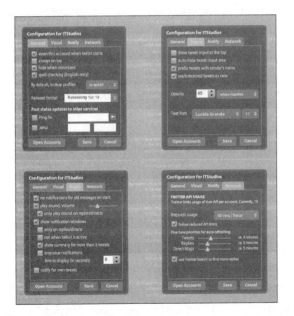

FIGURE 6.2 By single-clicking on the wrench, you can configure Twhirl to run the way that best suits you and your work environment. The various options for Twhirl are spread out across four tabs: General, Visual, Notify, and Network.

3. The Visual tab offers specifications for your tweets and Twitter interface by

> ▶ Placing the tweet input field at the top or bottom of the UI

> ▶ Offering auto-hide for the tweet field

> ▶ Identifying tweets by avatar, or by avatar and username

> ▶ Marking tweets as "new"

> ▶ Adjusting Twhirl's window opacity

> ▶ Selecting Twhirl's display font

Set up Visual to your specifications, and then proceed to the Notify tab.

4. Notify controls Twhirl's notification system. You can have your client

> ▶ Notify or not notify you of previous messages accumulated during down time when launching Twhirl

> ▶ Set volume for Twhirl's notification chimes, and whether to alert you on all new tweets or only @Replies

> ▶ Display small pop-up windows notifying you of feed activity

> ▶ Notify you on your own tweets

Set up Notify to your specifications, and then proceed to the Network tab.

5. The final tab is the Network tab in which you control the number of requests Twhirl makes from Twitter's servers. By increasing the delay between auto-refreshing, this equates to fewer requests per hour, thereby not exceeding your API limits. This also means more tweets to review depending on the size of your network.

6. Single-click the Save button to apply your configuration settings.

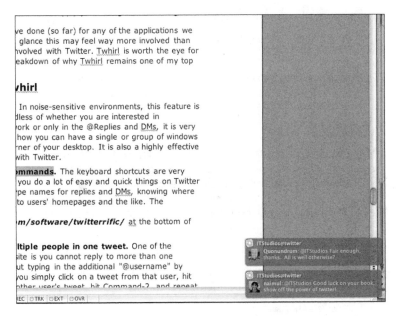

ve done (so far) for any of the applications we
glance this may feel way more involved than
nvolved with Twitter. Twhirl is worth the eye for
eakdown of why Twhirl remains one of my top

/hirl

In noise-sensitive environments, this feature is
dless of whether you are interested in
ork or only in the @Replies and DMs, it is very
how you can have a single or group of windows
ner of your desktop. It is also a highly effective
with Twitter.

mmands. The keyboard shortcuts are very
you do a lot of easy and quick things on Twitter
pe names for replies and DMs, knowing where
to users' homepages and the like. The

m/software/twitterrific/ at the bottom of

ltiple people in one tweet. One of the
site is you cannot reply to more than one
ut typing in the additional "@username" by
you simply click on a tweet from that user, hit
other user's tweet, hit Command-2, and repeat

FIGURE 6.3 Twhirl can be set up to send you @Replies and DMs as tiny pop-ups on your desktop, seen here alerting me while I'm in Microsoft Word.

Tweeting on Twhirl

With Twhirl appearing, behaving, and interfacing with Twitter.com the way we want it to, we are now ready to communicate with our network free of the confines of the homepage. From here, we can work as if we're directly tweeting from our Twitter.com, but right away you should notice a dramatic difference. Now you have access to all the various options for Twitter in one compact user interface.

1. At the bottom of Twhirl's window is a blank input field, your tweet field. (If your tweet field is not visible, click on the speech bubble icon located on the bottom-left corner, to the left of the Home button.) Single-click inside this field to type in the following tweet:

   This is my first tweet from Twhirl. @ITStudios is right – this client is pretty sharp! #twitterin10

As you type, a character countdown window keeps you updated on how many characters remain in your tweet.

2. To send your tweet, simply press the Return or Enter key on your keyboard, or single-click the Send Update icon (the single check mark) found below the character countdown.

WARNING

When you exceed Twitter's 140-character limit, the tweet field turns red, and Twhirl's counter goes into a negative number count, telling you how many characters you have exceeded. If you press Enter, Return, or the Send Update option, the tweet, stops at the 140-character point both in your Twitter archives and in other clients.

---

3. Review your network's tweets in Twhirl's main window. When you find someone you want to reply to, roll your cursor over the user's avatar. You will be offered four options:

▶ Reply (@)

▶ Direct Message (envelope)

▶ Favorite (heart)

▶ Retweet (>>)

Click on the Reply icon. The user's Twitter handle appears in the tweet field. Compose your reply and press Return, Enter, or the Send Update icon.

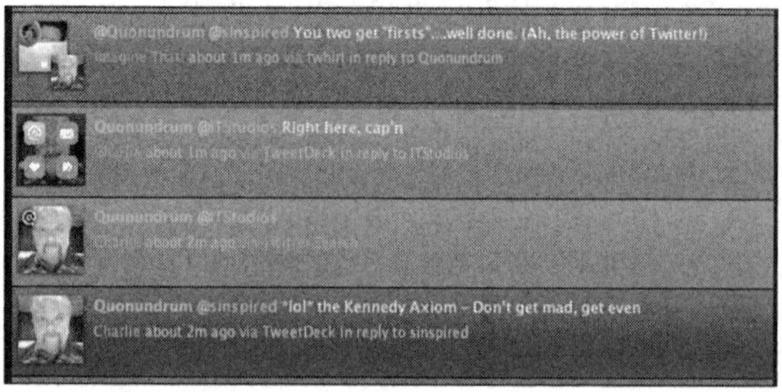

FIGURE 6.4 Hovering your mouse over a user's avatar (as seen in second Tweet from the top) offers four options: Send Reply, Send DM, Favorite, or Retweet.

Using Twhirl to Shorten URLs

Along with the capabilities of Twitter.com built into the interface, Twhirl also offers services that are found across the Internet. Here, we use Twhirl to shorten a URL.

1. Find a long URL (blogpost, webpage, and such), single-click the URL in your browser, and press either Command-A (Mac) or Control-A (PC) on your keyboard.

2. Press Command-C (Mac) or Control-C (PC) to copy the URL on to your clipboard.

3. In Twhirl, look for the Shorten URL icon (a chain link) located to the right of the tweet input field. Single-click the Shorten URL icon.

4. In the Shorten URL interface, paste the unaltered URL into the URL data field.

5. Single-click the Service menu to select the URL shortening website you want to use. You can choose from the following:

- ▶ http://is.gd

- ▶ http://bit.ly

- ▶ http://snurl.com

6. Single-click the Shorten button to create your condensed URL. It appears automatically in your tweet input field.

7. Compose your tweet and press Return, Enter, or the Send Update icon.

Twhirl is one impressive client and extremely powerful in what it does and how it does it. Many popular websites that enable users to incorporate various media with tweets can be accessed through Twhirl, including one of the most popular photo-sharing Twitter sites.

Using Twhirl to Share TwitPics

As discussed in Chapter 5, TwitPic is for users who want to distribute their photography across Twitter. This site invites users to upload their photos and share them with their respective networks. When users (logged into TwitPic) leave comments, a new tweet featuring the photo in question is generated and circulated on to other Twitter networks.

Twhirl offers its users the ability to upload and share photos through TwitPic without ever leaving the client's UI.

1. Compose a tweet that best describes the photo you want to share. (Make it brief because you want to leave room for the TwitPic URL.)

2. Underneath the Refresh icon is the Share an Image (a camera) icon. Single-click Share an Image and browse your computer for an image you want to share.

3. Click Select to prepare an image for uploading. In Twhirl's TwitPic window, a preview of the image appears, as shown in Figure 6.5. Single-click Post Image to begin the upload process.

FIGURE 6.5   After selecting an image, Twhirl renders a preview of the image you want to upload to TwitPic.

4. When the TwitPic URL appears, press Return, Enter, or the Send Update icon to make the post.

Twhirl uploads the photo on to your TwitPic account and retrieves from there a TwitPic URL, all from your desktop.

> **NOTE**
>
> When users comment on your TwitPics, the image is automatically shared on that user's network with their comment accompanying the TwitPic's URL.

Along with TwitPic, Twhirl can also access Twitter Search (covered in Chapter 4, "Tracking Trends and Traffic on Twitter") from your desktop and, much like subscribing to a search query via RSS, can alert you to any updates concerning previous search queries.

Using Twhirl to Perform Twitter Searches

Searching Twitter from Twhirl's UI is just as easy as uploading a picture to TwitPic using Twhirl. Once again, from the desktop, you can tap into the power of popular search engines to track terms and trends you are curious about.

1. In the Twhirl interface, the farthest right icon along the bottom of its user interface is a magnifying glass, tagged Search when you roll your cursor over it. Single-click on it to access Twitter Search.

2. Single-click the menu to the right of the input field. You can choose from the following to perform your query search on Twitter:

  ▶ Twitter Search

  ▶ TweetScan

Make sure Twitter Search is selected.

3. Type your search term into the data field and press Return or Enter on your keyboard. Your results appear in your Twhirl window.

NOTE

Offered with Twitter Search is a similar tool called TweetScan (http://tweetscan.com). Resembling the same setup as Twitter Search, only with a Search Cloud at the homepage displaying the most recent and popular search terms, you can follow the same steps for TweetScan as you do for Twitter Search. When your query hits appear, you can also subscribe to the search results via RSS by clicking on the RSS link in the upper-right corner of the search results. If you prefer TweetScan over Twitter Search, feel free to select it in step 2. TweetScan becomes your default setting for Twhirl's Search option unless you switch it back to Twitter Search.

---

4. In the top-right corner of the Twhirl window, you see an Activate button. Single-clicking this button stores this search term and searches it when accessed, similar to subscribing to a query via your RSS reader. When new instances of this search occur, you find them by accessing Twhirl's Search window, as shown in Figure 6.6.

Twhirl brings with its simple, compact interface a wide variety of Twitter options to your desktop. It is best used when first starting out and can help economize your time and attention between Twitter and the rest of the web. Hopping from service to service and site to site is now (thanks in part to Adobe AIR) localized to your desktop.

But can you outgrow Twhirl? After cracking beyond 1,000 followers, Twhirl can be difficult to use because your main feed fills the window quickly. Twitter networks can reach a level in which an application such as Twhirl just isn't enough. What is needed for users reaching into the thousands is a remote client that can not only retrieve new tweets but also organize followers into various categories of your making, while still tracking search queries and trends that catch your interest.

For this kind of power, users turn to TweetDeck.

FIGURE 6.6 Twitter Search in Twhirl enables you to not only access the power of Twitter Search remotely from your desktop, but also enables you to store previous searches for later access.

LESSON 7

Using Third-Party Applications: TweetDeck

In July 2008, an application intending to fulfill the needs of Twitter accounts sporting larger-than-average communities debuted; and within months, this client quickly gained popularity. Along with aiding Twitter users in cultivating massive numbers, this application also helped with users that tweeted frequently and took advantage of various online utilities. Some power users swear by it whereas certain early-adopter circles loathe its intent to filter out certain voices. Whatever argument you take or make, it is impossible to ignore or deny the influence (and popularity) of TweetDeck (http://tweetdeck.com) within the Twitter community.

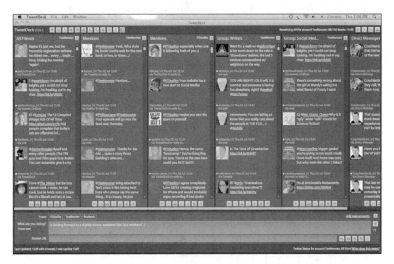

FIGURE 7.1 For Twitter's power users, TweetDeck gives you the ability to organize your Followers in categories, with other options built in the application.

It is not uncommon to see a familiar "Giving TweetDeck a try...." tweet. What is most telling about the new users of TweetDeck are how they compare TweetDeck to Twhirl. Both applications share similar options, but the final decision on whether you use TweetDeck depends on the size of your network. For the Twitter user that develops a network into the thousands, TweetDeck is a powerhouse that helps you get things done in Twitter.

Installation and Initial Setup of TweetDeck

Similar to Twhirl and other third-party applications, TweetDeck needs Adobe AIR installed before it can get to work. Without Adobe AIR, TweetDeck can't run. Follow http://get.adobe.com/air to Adobe AIR's download page on Adobe.com.

1. If you haven't already, download a copy of Adobe AIR and install it on your computer. When verified, return to TweetDeck's homepage and download the latest version.

2. Install TweetDeck and follow login procedures for your account. You do not need to be logged out of Twitter to log on with TweetDeck.

3. When you initially log in, TweetDeck's tweet field and main interface is located at the top of the screen. If you want your tweet field located at the bottom of the screen, click on the wrench icon to access your Settings. Under the General tab, make sure these options—along with the tweet at the bottom of the screen—are also checked

   ▶ Have a Notification Window appear at the top of your (primary) monitor to let you know of new tweets.

   ▶ Play your computer's alert sound on receiving new tweets.

   ▶ Open user profiles and shared photos in external browsers as opposed to within TweetDeck.

   ▶ Auto include hashtags when replying to tweets.

   As for the other options feature, feel free to explore what they do or pick up *All a Twitter* for a more in-depth look at what they offer.

4. The Twitter API tab is like Twhirl's Network tab in which your requests to Twitter per hour (your Twitter API limits) are set. You can increase or decrease the delay between auto-refreshing or turn off Twitter updates all together by single-clicking the Turn Off Twitter Updates button. The Total percentage number you see is how "close" you are cutting it with your current settings to your API limits. After you set your limits to settings that work best for you, click on the Services tab.

NOTE

By default, your API Limits are set to 75 percent. Although that is fine for the average user, for power users who have thousands (or tens of thousands) in their network, it is easy to exceed the default setting and slam the brakes on your tweeting habits. I recommend resetting your API limits (based on the combination of delays that work best for you) to fall between 50 percent to 60 percent to decrease the amount of your requests to Twitter, thereby staying well within your set limits.

5. For Twitter users who manage more than one username, versions of TweetDeck v0.26.3 and up offer support for tweeting across multiple accounts. Click on the Accounts tab and enter a new Twitter account and password. Click the Add Account button and, when verified, you can access these other Twitter accounts.

NOTE

When tweeting across multiple accounts, simply click on the account name featured just above the "Compose Tweet" field. The account will remain active until you click on it again. Clicking on a tweet to reply or DM will automatically activate that account, but keep an eye to see if you have other active accounts. You might be posting across multiple IDs without realizing it.

6. In the same window (Accounts), you can also enter into TweetDeck your Facebook account. After access is verified, your TweetDeck posts can also appear as Facebook status updates.

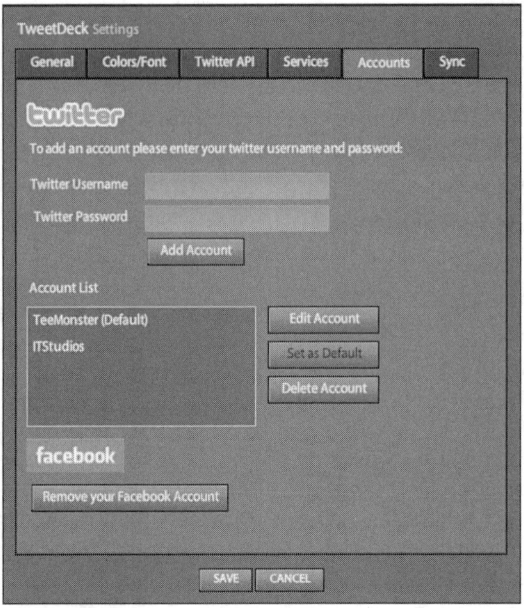

FIGURE 7.2   In TweetDeck, users can now access and manage multiple accounts and update their Facebook status.

7. Click on the Sync tab to set up a TweetDeck account. If you do not have a TweetDeck account, simply provide an email address and create a password.

    The TweetDeck account remembers special groups you have set up across multiple Twitter accounts and enables you to import in custom columns and search queries. Your TweetDeck account is like TweetDeck itself: It's free.

With your account(s) now up and running on TweetDeck, you are about to get deep into its features, including tweeting across multiple usernames and setting up specialized columns for organizational purposes. When you have your followers organized and set up TweetDeck to track more than just one username, you will soon understand how this application became such a major player in the Twitterverse.

Setting Up Groups in TweetDeck

Arguably, TweetDeck's strongest asset is its option to organize members of a network into individual *Groups*. When you establish groups, a new column is created, and then this new group simply waits on you to add members to it accordingly.

1. In the top-left corner of your TweetDeck window, you have a toolbar of features. (A *lot* of them.) From left to right, the tools that we will focus on, here and throughout this book, are

   ▶ Access Tweet Field (speech bubble)

   ▶ View All Friends (globe)

   ▶ View @Mentions (curved arrow)

   ▶ View Direct Messages (envelope)

   ▶ Create Groups (User-User)

   ▶ Twitter Search (magnifying glass)

   ▶ View 12Seconds updates (12)

   ▶ View Facebook Updates in separate column (the Facebook icon)

   You can single-click these tools to create new columns featuring various feeds for your account.

   Now, single-click on the Create Group icon. Your tweet field collapses, and a window appears to the right side showing all active members of your Twitter network.

2. In the Add New Group window, give your group a name.

3. Scroll through your network and check those Followers that best fit this grouping. After you finish designating members of this group, single-click the Save Group button.

4. TweetDeck creates a new column featuring your group. Double-clicking on the group name accesses the group, and you can add to the group and change the group's name if you like. You can also arrange your columns by going to the toolbar at the bottom of your group's column and single-clicking the Move Column Left button (the left arrow icon) or the Move Column Right button (the right arrow icon).

FIGURE 7.3 The Add New Group option offers you the ability to create (or edit) a group's name (that is, Family, Coworkers, Gaming Club, and so on) and include (or remove) followers.

WARNING

While you create new groups, TweetDeck still receives your feed. If a tweet appears that strikes your nerve to reply or retweet, **don't.** If you do before finishing your group, TweetDeck closes the Save Group window without saving any of the changes you made.

---

5. If you receive a tweet from someone that should be in one of your groups, click on her username to pull up a Profile window. At the bottom of this window are two options: Unfollow and Add a Group (User-User icon). Click on Add a Group, select the group or groups you want this user associated with and then close the window.

FIGURE 7.4 In a new window, TweetDeck can access user profile details and follow options, and has the ability to organize new or current followers into groups.

Within minutes of setting up columns and groups, you can begin tweeting with this powerful desktop application. TweetDeck, as it has been mentioned, is particularly good for Twitter users who manage multiple accounts. With a few quick clicks, you can easily float from one username to another, or with a single post tweet across your accounts and even update your Facebook status.

Tweeting from TweetDeck

Depending on your preferences, your tweet field will either be at the top or bottom of the TweetDeck UI. You might think tweeting is the same from application to application; however, TweetDeck does things a little differently, particularly when it comes to the multiple account support.

1. Log into TweetDeck (if you haven't already) and review your incoming tweets.

2. In the open tweet field, begin typing your message. To the far-right of your field, you see the character counter. (If the tweet field goes red, you have exceeded your limit.) Feel free to use this as a tweet:

Currently giving TweetDeck a try, on the advice of @ITStudios. #twitterin10

When your tweet is ready, press the Return or Enter key to send your tweet.

3. Similar to Twhirl, when you roll over an avatar of a user, you are given the following options to choose.

   ▶ Reply (curved arrow)

   ▶ Direct Message (envelope)

   ▶ Retweet (arrow)

   ▶ Other Options (gear)

   Click on any of these options to either be prompted to reply to someone or retweet another member's tweet.

4. Find a tweet with a hashtag and click the Reply feature. If the preference is checked, the hashtag is automatically included with your reply. Enter in your reply and press Send.

5. Begin composing a new tweet in TweetDeck. When you are done, take a look at your UI. Single-click the icon with the pound sign (#) located at the far right of the tweet field. This hashtag feature keeps track of recent hashtags you have either used or tweeted with. If applicable, select a hashtag from the list. The hashtag appears in your tweet.

6. If you have a Facebook account and multiple Twitter accounts, single-click on the buttons labeled "facebook" and with your other user names. As seen in Figure 7.5, the accounts you are tweeting on will be highlighted. Compose a tweet in TweetDeck and press Return or Enter. Your tweet is not only sent across your multiple accounts, but your Facebook status is also updated.

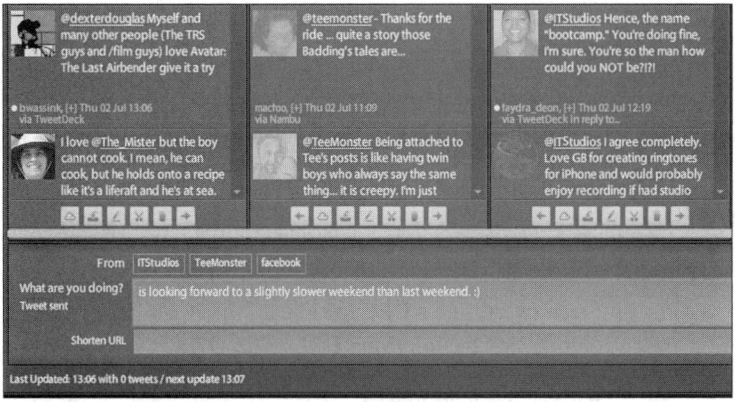

FIGURE 7.5   From TweetDeck, your Facebook status can be updated along with multiple Twitter feeds, all with a single tweet.

WARNING

The ability to tweet across multiple accounts is extremely handy, but it is also easy to forget you have enabled this feature. Make sure to check which accounts are active, and that you are not inundating users who follow you across several accounts with tweets. Constant cross-posting and frequent Facebook updates smacks a bit of spam.

TweetDeck, along with its modest Facebook integration, also offers integration with other online Twitter utilities. With a better understanding of how these utilities work and what they do, TweetDeck offers you options to tap into its capabilities, all from the comfort of one interface, one application.

Using TweetDeck to Shorten URLs

Discussed earlier in this book are the websites out there that shorten URLs dramatically, thereby saving the valuable characters we need to communicate with on Twitter. With TweetDeck, you do not even need to use copy-and-paste to apply your URL. Everything is taken care of in the UI.

1. Log into TweetDeck (if you haven't already) and review your incoming tweets.

2. In the open tweet field, begin typing your message. You can compose one of your own choice or use this one:

   @ITStudios talking about "The Trouble with Twitter."

   Then place your cursor before the hashtag (if you have one). *Do not send the tweet right now.*

3. For your own tweet, find a URL to include with it. Or if you use the tweet I supply, visit the following URL on YouTube:

   http://www.youtube.com/watch?v=SHv7b7can60&feature=related

   You can also search YouTube under the following search parameters:

   ▶ ANTI-Social Media

   ▶ Twitter

   ▶ Tee Morris

   When you find your link, go to your browser, and from its URL field, select the URL by pressing Control+A (Windows) or Command-A (Mac), and then copy it by pressing Control+C (Windows) or Command-C (Mac).

4. Return to your TweetDeck UI and below the tweet field is a Shorten URL field. Paste in the URL you copied by pressing Control+V (Windows) or Command-V (Mac) into the Shorten URL field, as shown in Figure 7.6.

FIGURE 7.6 To shorten a URL in TweetDeck's UI, take your destination URL and paste it into the Shorten URL field (above). Click on the Shorten URL icon (circled in top) to condense and insert it into your tweet (below).

5. Also shown in Figure 7.6 are a series of small icons to the right of the Shorten URL field. These icons are online utilities you can remotely use from TweetDeck. The first option (two arrows pointing at each other) is the Shorten URL option. Single-click this option to shorten the URL and drop it into your tweet.

NOTE

As a shortcut, you can instantly shorten a URL and send it by pasting the URL into the Shorten URL field and pressing the Return or Enter key. In one stroke, the URL is shortened and sent.

---

6. Add in a hashtag of your making (or "#twitterin10" if you use my tweet and URL here) and then press Enter or Return to send your tweet.

7. Single-click the Settings option and in this window, click on the Services tab. Next to the option Select the Service You Wish to Use to Shorten URLs, you can single-click the URL utility you prefer:

- ▶ bit.ly
- ▶ digg
- ▶ is.gd
- ▶ tinyurl
- ▶ tr.im
- ▶ twurl

Select it from the menu, as seen in Figure 7.7, and then click.

Shortening URLs is one of the many features TweetDeck brings to you. Uploading and sharing photographs is also just as easy.

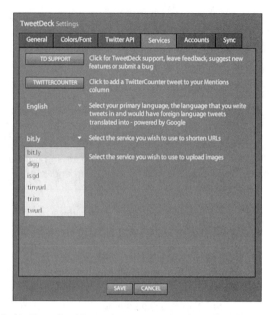

FIGURE 7.7   In TweetDeck's settings, you can select the URL utility you pre-fer.

Using TwitPic with TweetDeck

In Chapter 5, "Incorporating Media with Twitter," I mention TwitPic, the first of many online options offered for sharing photos with your Twitter network. TwitPic's reputation for its services earned it the support of many third-party applications such as TweetDeck, and TweetDeck makes sharing media via TwitPic a snap.

1. Log into TweetDeck (if you haven't already) and review your incoming tweets.

2. Single-click the Settings option and in this window, click on the Services tab. Next to the option Select the Service You Wish to Use to Upload Images, you can single-click the URL utility you prefer.

   ▶ TwitPic

   ▶ YFrog

Select or confirm that TwitPic is selected, and then click it to return to the Settings window. Then click the Save option.

3. Return to your TweetDeck UI and below the tweet field, in the row of various options where Shorten URL is located, is the Upload a Photo (camera) option. Single-click it to access the Upload a Photo interface.

NOTE

When you use multiple accounts on Twitter, you will be prompted to select an account to use with TwitPic. From the drop-down menu provided, select the account you want to use and then click Select Account to proceed.

---

4. From the Select file window, find an image you want to share and then single-click the Select button.

5. To the left of the tweet field, you will be notified that image is uploading. When the upload is complete, you will be given notification as to whether the upload was successful. If successful, your tweet field gets a TwitPic URL, as shown in Figure 7.8.

FIGURE 7.8 After uploading an image, TweetDeck informs you that you have successfully uploaded a picture and then creates a TwitPic URL for you.

6. Compose a complete tweet around your newly created TwitPic address and then send.

Your link is now shared with your network and can be viewed by everyone. People can retweet your link in TweetDeck, or comment on your picture at TwitPic and automatically generate another tweet as an @Mention to you.

With laptops and smartphones pre-installed with webcams and the ease of digital video editing, TweetDeck is working on integrating media exchanges other than still images. TweetDeck also offers notification, playback, and distribution of short video snippets.

Using 12seconds.tv with TweetDeck

Also featured in Chapter 5, with TwitPic, MobyPicture, and others, is the video sharing site, 12seconds.tv (http://12Seconds.tv). It promises you exactly what you think: a free, 12-second platform to speak your mind. TweetDeck offers you some integration, both in the sending and in the tracking of followers on 12seconds.tv.

1. Log into TweetDeck (if you haven't already) and review your incoming tweets.

2. Single-click the "12" icon at the top of your screen to access your 12seconds.tv account.

NOTE

To access 12seconds.tv through TweetDeck, you need to have an active 12seconds.tv account. You can create one for free either through TweetDeck or by going to http://12seconds.tv. For details on 12seconds.tv, take a look at Chapter 5.

---

3. TweetDeck creates a new column called 12seconds.tv. The interface for the column is different from other TweetDeck columns. You have two options for the 12seconds.tv column:

   ▶ Move Column Left (arrow)

   ▶ Record (a single dot)

   Consider a 12-second message you'd like to share and then single-click the Record option.

4. A window pops up, confirming your webcam preferences. When you have everything set, click the record button. 12seconds.tv gives you a preview window and a countdown of what you are recording.

NOTE

If playback and/or recording is a challenge for you, try visiting http://12seconds.tv and see if you can record and playback there. If prompted, upgrade your Flash plug-in and try again, both at the main site and via TweetDeck.

5. When you have recorded your 12 seconds of video, either single-click Cancel to re-record the message, the X in the top-right corner to close the window completely, or Post It to submit the video.

6. After single-clicking Post It you will be prompted to give details on your video. Fill in the details and then single-click the Submit button.

FIGURE 7.9   You can play videos from 12seconds.tv through TweetDeck by single-clicking on their respective thumbnails.

NOTE

12seconds.tv on TweetDeck does not enable you to upload videos from your hard drive, only record live. To upload video from your computer, you need to use the 12seconds.tv interface.

7. Your recent 12 seconds post on the website and then appear in
TweetDeck on the next refresh. To view it or any of the videos
featured in the 12seconds.tv column, single-click on the thumbnail of the video. The window, as shown in Figure 7.9, appears
and automatically plays the selected video.

This is how easy it is to share video across your Twitter network. 12sec-
onds.tv is, as mentioned in Chapter 5, a Social Networking site similar to
Twitter only with video. TweetDeck works exceptionally well as a bridge
between both networks, allowing 12seconds.tv users to tap into their
Twitter network and vice versa.

Performing a Twitter Search with TweetDeck

A feature in many Twitter clients is the integration of Twitter Search into
their interfaces. TweetDeck combines two features of Twitter Search into
one command and keeps you informed on who is talking about your interests.

1. Log into TweetDeck (if you haven't already) and review your
incoming tweets.

2. Single-click the magnifying glass icon at the top of your screen
to access the Twitter Search window. Type in the term, phrase, or
hashtag you want to track.

NOTE

To perform a Twitter Search with hashtags, make sure you remember
the pound sign (#) when you perform the search. Make sure you
also spell the hashtag properly.

3. Figure 7.10 is an example of Twitter Search results through
TweetDeck. A new column labeled with your Search query is
created with a notification of your results appearing briefly.

FIGURE 7.10   A new column appears in TweetDeck when you perform a search. TweetDeck tracks in this column any new mentions of your Search query.

4. If you leave the column open and running, your results update any time a tweet appears fitting your query.

5. Closing the column shuts down that search, but you can always access that query by repeating step 1. To the right of the Search window's entry field, you see a drop-down menu of previous searches. Select the one you want to create a new column in TweetDeck.

In this chapter you can see that when it comes to desktop clients, TweetDeck carries the kind of impact that Wile E. Coyote would feel when the anvil dropped from the pulley: TweetDeck packs quite a lasting impact. With every upgrade, it continues to evolve and impress users and is regarded by many power users as the must-have application in a Twitter arsenal. Go exploring and take a closer look at what TweetDeck can do for you. Just make sure to hold on to something. This client will definitely take you for one wild ride!

Using Twitter on the Android G1

Twitter is all about connecting with friends and colleagues, being in the know, and being kept in the loop. It is, though, a bizarre addiction. This addiction becomes noticeable when you step away from your computer. Time seems to creep by. Fingertips itch for the feel of a keyboard. The world around you seems a bit more quiet.

Fortunately, to feed this addiction, there are Twitter clients for mobile phones. Now, if you have a data connection, you have the ability to tweet.

WARNING

Before tweeting from your favorite mobile device, take a moment to look at your surroundings. If you are waiting for the local metro rail or enjoying a cup of coffee in a café, by all means, start tweeting. In **social** situations—family gatherings, evenings with a significant other, the movies, and such—losing yourself in Twitter might come across a bit rude. Consider the time and place before tweeting on the go.

One of the most recent smartphones offering Twitter across wireless data networks is the T-Mobile-Google-HTC collaboration, the *Android G1* (or HTC Dream for some overseas clientele, or more commonly referred to as the Google Phone, found online at http://www.androidg1.org). First appearing on the market in late-2008, the Google Phone offers cool iPhone-esque features such as the touch-screen interface but also offers a BlackBerry-inspired slide keyboard that keeps the phone streamlined, compact, and easy to handle.

FIGURE 8.1 The Android G1, or Google Phone, offers on its open source Android operating system Twitter on the go through a variety of applications.

TwitterRide for the G1

TwitterRide is found at http://twitterride.net and describes itself as "a simple and fast Twitter client for your Android G1." It is a free download for G1 users, and client engineer Satoshi Tanimoto manages to emulate the look and feel of a full Twitter client while keeping the performance fast.

Twitter's most basic of functions are included.

- ▶ Create new tweets, @Mentions, and DMs in a tweet field at the top of its interface.

- ▶ Receive tweets, @Mentions, and DMs from Followers.

- ▶ Access User Profiles (through URL to Twitter homepage).

- ▶ Integrate with Android's gallery for sharing, uploading, and tweeting via TwitPic.

- ▶ Quick access to Trends and Search Twitter.

FIGURE 8.2   TwitterRide modestly calls itself a "simple and fast" G1 client, but it performs with all the capabilities of a desktop client.

As these features are expected from any Twitter client, TwitterRide offers a few more incentives:

▶ Built-in version checker to alert users of upgrades (which can be deactivated in Preferences)

▶ Auto-refresh runs when you post a new tweet

▶ "Nearby" feature offered in GUI

▶ Favorites management

▶ Background notifications (similar to Twhirl) for replies and direct messages that also work as a shortcut to TwitterRide

▶ Advanced features (such as a Follow/Unfollow option) offered when accessing User Profile

So, for a "simple and fast client" TwitterRide does bring a lot to your G1. Let's take a quick tour of the basics.

Setting Up TwitterRide

1. On your G1, launch the Android Market and search for "twitter-ride" to download and install your copy.

2. When installed, launch TwitterRide. Enter your username and your password in the provided fields when prompted. Tap Verify Credentials to check your username and password.

3. Background Notification is similar to Figure 6.3 in Chapter 6, "Using Third-Party Applications: Twhirl," of this book. On your main screen or in another G1 application, a small note appears in the notification bar to let you know a tweet has arrived for you. You can have TwitterRide operate in this mode by selecting the Check for New Statuses When Application Is Not Running option.

4. TwitterRide enables you to use your G1 as a notification device. Scroll down in this menu to select Notify for Replies and Messages Only to have the G1's built-in alerts notify you.

5. From this same menu, as shown in Figure 8.3, select from the following notification options:

   ▶ Vibration (TwitterRide vibrates the G1.)

   ▶ LED Flash (TwitterRide uses the G1's power indicator.)

   ▶ Ringtone (TwitterRide uses the current G1 ringtone.)

6. Tap Save to continue into the TwitterRide GUI.

TwitterRide now runs the way you want it to run, even tapping into the built-in notification systems of your Google phone. Now that we're in the UI, let's send our first mobile tweet.

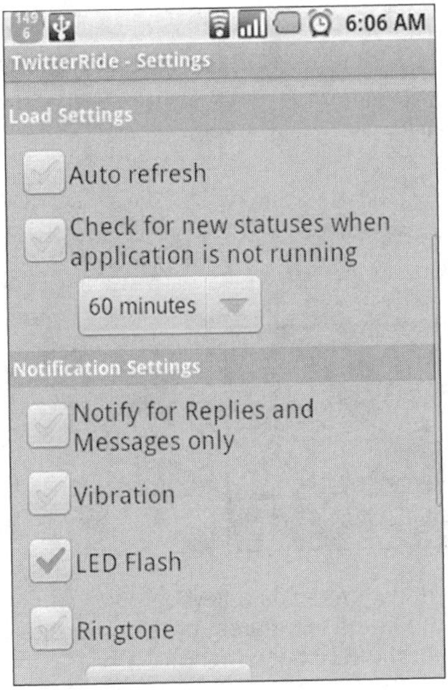

FIGURE 8.3 At the initial login window, TwitterRide offers different preferences, including using the G1 as a notification device.

Tweeting Using TwitterRide

1. After previous tweets have loaded, click the Menu button on your G1 to access the main menu for TwitterRide. Select the Post option to compose a tweet.

2. As in many other Twitter applications, compose your tweet here (using either an on-screen keyboard seen on the left in Figure 8.4; or the attached keyboard of your G1 phone), keeping an eye on the character countdown, located in the lower-left corner of the interface.

3. When the tweet is ready, tap the Send option on your screen.

4. To reply to someone in your network, simply tap on that person's tweet and then select either the @Reply or DM option in the Post interface.

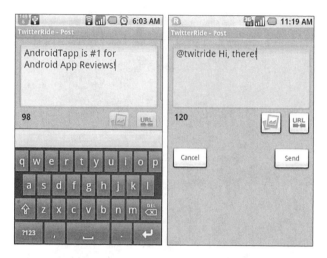

FIGURE 8.4 TwitterRide offers you a keyboard you work in vertical mode (left) with a single tap in the input area, or removes the keyboard if you use the one included with the G1 phone (right).

And that's all there is to tweeting directly from an Android G1!

At a glance, though, you should catch some of the other features of TwitterRide. As intuitive and easy as it was for us to get TwitterRide up and running, the UI makes it equally easy for those wanting to do more than just tweet-and-run to go beyond the basic post and reply.

Sharing Photos with TwitterRide

1. Launch TwitterRide. Enter your username and your password in the provided fields when prompted. Tap Verify Credentials to check your username and password, and continue into TwitterRide's GUI. After tweets have loaded, review your feed.

2. Click the Menu button on your G1 to access the main menu for TwitterRide. Select the Post option to compose a tweet or @Replies to reply to another user.

3. After you compose a tweet here, tap the Add Photo (the two photographs) icon. TwitterRide takes you into your G1's Photo Gallery, pictured in Figure 8.5. You can select a photo for uploading by tapping on a thumbnail and tapping the Upload

button, or you can take a picture with your G1's camera by tapping the Camera button.

FIGURE 8.5   Tapping the Add Photo feature takes you into your G1 Gallery
in which you can either upload a photo or take a picture for uploading to
TwitPic.

NOTE

TwitterRide uses TwitPic as its photo sharing service. After you tap
Upload or take a picture with the G1 camera, the image is uploaded
to TwitPic.com. For more on TwitPic, see Chapter 5, "Incorporating
Media with Twitter."

---

   4. When the tweet is ready (with the TwitPic URL added), tap the
   Send option on your screen.

TwitterRide emulates the desktop experience with features such as
TwitPic integration, tracking of trending topics, and Twitter Searches of
hashtags.

And, of course, to preserve those precious characters, TwitterRide does include integration with a popular URL utility.

Condensing URLs with TwitterRide

1. Launch TwitterRide. Enter your username and your password in the provided fields when prompted. Tap Verify Credentials to check your username and password, and continue into TwitterRide's GUI. After tweets have loaded, review your feed.

> **NOTE**
>
> You can, in TwitterRide's Settings, save your credential information so that you do not need to continue repeating the log in process.

2. Click the Menu button on your G1 to access the main menu for TwitterRide. Select the Post option to compose a tweet or @Replies to reply to another user.

3. After you compose a tweet here, tap the Add URL (URL over a chain link) icon. Figure 8.6 shows the Add URL Interface that is a combination of both a URL entry field and a URL shortener. Using the on-screen keyboard, the keyboard connected with your phone, or the G1's Paste function, you can enter a URL into the available field.

> **NOTE**
>
> TwitterRide uses Bit.ly as its URL condenser. For more on Bit.ly and its tracking capabilities, see Chapter 4, "Tracking Trends and Traffic on Twitter."

4. Tap the Insert button to accept and shorten the URL with Bit.ly. The URL is automatically incorporated into your tweet. You can also exit this option without incorporating any URL by tapping the Cancel button.

5. When the tweet is ready (with the shortened URL added), tap the Send option on your screen.

FIGURE 8.6   TwitterRide's Add URL function automatically shortens your URL and incorporates it into your tweet.

6. Find your new tweet in TwitterRide's Friends viewing option. Copy the shortened URL you just created.

7. Use your G1 to get on the web, and paste the Bit.ly URL into the URL field, adding a + after it. You can now track your link's traffic using your Google phone.

NOTE

When browsing the web on the G1, you can share a page you're visiting directly to TwitterRide.

With the popularity of smartphones and wireless data networks, it comes as no surprise that Twitter is now accessible anywhere thanks to developers like Tanimoto and applications like TwitterRide. The Google phone and TwitterRide are only the beginning as other popular smartphones have their own compact Twitter clients, all striving to bring users as close to the desktop experience as possible while they tweet desktop-free.

Using Twitter on the BlackBerry

First introduced in 1999 and revolutionizing in 2002 wireless data transfer and communications, the *BlackBerry* (http://na.blackberry.com/eng/) brags an impressive following of more than 28 million (so says Wikipedia!), one of them America's 44th president, Barack Obama. The BlackBerry was *the first* mobile phone to be dubbed a *smartphone* and offers its own server for integration into a company's corporate network.

FIGURE 9.1 The BlackBerry (their latest model, Storm, pictured here) first introduced to the market a mobile phone that went far beyond what phones of the day could do.

It stands to reason that Twitter would find a place on the BlackBerry, the pioneer of the smartphone movement. As previously mentioned, you can use an SMS option to receive tweets, but as the BlackBerry uses data networks (3G, for example) to communicate, the SMS feature is a step back. Smartphone takes its users *on* the Internet; and just as was seen in Chapter 8, "Using Twitter on the Android G1," with the Google phone, tweeting from your phone acts almost as if you never left your desktop computer.

TwitterBerry for the BlackBerry

If you want to gauge the popularity of this application, simply ask on Twitter, *"Is anyone tweeting on a BlackBerry? If so, what do you use?"* Watch how many replies you receive that name TwitterBerry (http://orangatame.com/products/twitterberry/).

At least in my Twitter networks, TwitterBerry stands as the most popular client for the BlackBerry. Provided you run BlackBerry OS 4.1.0+ (or OS 4.2+ for TwitPic support) and connect to the Internet via BlackBerry Internet Browsing Service, a BlackBerry Enterprise Server, or a direct data connection, this free client offers full integration with Twitter and TwitPic.

A single-click of the trackball brings up the main menu in TwitterBerry, offering you these options:

- ▶ Update your feed.
- ▶ View Friends Timeline.
- ▶ View @Mention.
- ▶ View Direct Messages.
- ▶ Review Friends List.
- ▶ Show Full Menu.

The Full Menu option also displays

- ▶ Public Timeline (that is, everyone)
- ▶ Your Account's Timeline
- ▶ Sent Direct Messages

▶ TwitterBerry Preferences

▶ Application Information (running version, developers, etc.)

FIGURE 9.2   Twitterberry, from Orangatame brings many features of desktop Twitter clients to your Blackberry.

Getting Started with TwitterBerry

Downloading and installing TwitterBerry takes only a minute or two, depending on the speed of your data connection. After it's installed, let's explore some of its capabilities.

1. On your BlackBerry, launch your browser and visit http://orangatame.com/products/twitterberry/ to download and install TwitterBerry. Upon launching TwitterBerry, you are asked to log into Twitter. Do so.

2. You are automatically sent to the default Twitter welcome screen, asking, *"What are you doing?"* Compose your first mobile tweet in the open field using your BlackBerry's keyboard.

3. Click on the BlackBerry's trackball or Menu button to access TwitterBerry's main menu. Select Update to send your tweet.

NOTE

You might notice on feature-rich, graphic intensive clients like TwitterBerry that your BlackBerry might slow down in performance when compared to desktop client Twitter.com. Keep in mind that the performance of your mobile client, whatever platform you're on, will be based on the speed of your smartphone's data network.

FIGURE 9.3 By clicking on the Full Menu option, TwitterBerry gives you more options to choose from for your tweeting tendencies.

4. Click the BlackBerry's trackball or Menu button to access the main menu again. Click on the Full Menu option to access other features of TwitterBerry.

5. From the full menu select Get Replies that fetches only those tweets that contain @Mentions of your username.

6. Scroll over your messages using the trackball. Find a message you'd like to reply to, single-click the trackball, and from the menu select Reply to compose and send your tweet.

7. From the full menu access Friends Timeline to review only your friends. Scroll over your messages using the trackball and find a

message you'd need to tweet privately. Single-click the trackball, and from the menu select Direct Message to compose and send your tweet.

8. Click the BlackBerry's trackball or Menu button to access the main menu again. Scroll over your messages using the trackball and find a message that is one you want to keep. Single-click the trackball, and select Favorite to mark that tweet as a favorite of yours.

These are the basics in tweeting with TwitterBerry. You now have what you need to reply, DM, and keep your network in the know. Beyond basic communication, TwitterBerry also offers many of the additional options found in popular desktop clients.

Sharing Photos with TwitterBerry

1. Exit TwitterBerry and head over to your Media Gallery.

2. Find an image you want to share with your Twitter network, select it, and then access your menu. You should now see Send to TwitterBerry at the top of your options. Select it.

FIGURE 9.4 Tapping the Add Photo feature takes you into your G1 Gallery where you can either upload a photo or take a picture for uploading to TwitPic.

3. Exit your gallery and return to TwitterBerry. When you reach the welcome screen (seen in step 2 of "Getting Started with TwitterBerry"), your image is attached at the bottom of the screen. Compose your tweet and select Update from the menu.

> **NOTE**
>
> TwitterBerry uses TwitPic as its photo sharing service. When you tap Upload or take a picture with your BlackBerry, the image is uploaded to TwitPic.com after you update your tweet. For more on TwitPic, see Chapter 5, "Incorporating Media with Twitter."

Condensing URLs with TwitterBerry

1. Launch TwitterBerry. Enter your username and your password in the provided fields when prompted. From the Full menu select your Friends Timeline or Public Timeline, and review your incoming tweets.

2. Return to the main "splash page" and compose a tweet using a URL, either copied from your BlackBerry's browser or simply composed from memory.

3. Bring up your Menu and select the Update option.

4. If you review My Timeline from the Full menu, you note that your URL has been automatically shortened.

> **NOTE**
>
> The BlackBerry Storm can take your TwitterBerry experience and display it in a landscape mode. Turn your Storm either left or right, and the Storm resets the user interface to fit the new widescreen layout.

FIGURE 9.5 BlackBerry Storm users can now enjoy easier on-screen typing by using the mobile client in a landscape mode.

TwitterBerry provides for its users the ability to tweet and exchange images and URLs as efficiently and effectively as many desktop clients. It continues to be the popular client with BlackBerry users for its stability and ease of use. Now your tweets can continue uninterrupted while on the road with your smartphone; but keep in mind that although it is great to be portable, not every place is the appropriate place for Twitter. Whether it is behind the wheel of a moving vehicle or a social situation in which real-time conversation is key, always consider your surroundings before firing up TwitterBerry.

If, however, you are waiting for a train or enjoying a morning's best at a local coffee shop, enjoy Twitter away from your computer. It's almost like being there.

LESSON 10

Using Twitter on the iPhone

The iPhone (http://iphone.com), with its touch-and-drag interface and its ease of use, changed everything in the way smartphones were designed and interfaced with their users, interacting with their lives. iPhone users are as passionate about their phones as Mac users are passionate about their computers (present company included!), and tens of thousands of applications are available at the iTunes Application Store.

FIGURE 10.1 From Apple and AT&T comes the iPhone, one of the hottest innovations in wireless technology.

Some of these iPhone apps are designed for Social Networking and are made to bring Twitter to you iPhone-style.

Twittelator Pro for the iPhone

One of *Wall Street Journal*'s "16 Hottest New Releases" (Aug. 3, 2009) for the iPhone is a favorite of mine: *Twittelator,* from Stone Design (http://www.stone.com) and available in a free Lite version, or in a Pro version for USD$4.99. This application not only endeavors to bring many features of desktop clients to your iPhone but also brings users a few exclusive features not found anywhere else.

As shown in Figure 10.2, there is a slight difference between the Free version and the Pro. A comprehensive comparison between the two is at http://www.stone.com/Twittelator/Pro_versus_Lite_Features.html where the 90 (yes, nine-zero-*ninety*) exclusive Pro options can be considered.

FIGURE 10.2   Offered as both a paid and free download, Twittelator (Pro version's interface on left, Free on the right) brings to your iPhone a fully loaded Twitter experience.

Setting Up Twittelator Pro

Some of the exercises I will be featuring here are exclusive to the Pro version. (I like the Lite version, but I *use* the Pro.) When you first launch

Twittelator, you go through a login commonly found in many Twitter clients. You can apply the setup here with just about any iPhone app that brings Twitter to you, but from the point of login, we delve into features exclusive to Twittelator.

1. After purchase, download, and installation, launch Twittelator Pro, enter in your username and password, and then touch the Done button in the lower-right corner.

2. Your tweets are then gathered from your network and organized as "most recent" at the top to "oldest" at the bottom. You can scroll along your Timeline by dragging your finger vertically along the center of your screen.

3. Before tweeting, take a look at the menu bar across the bottom. You can find the following options:

> ▶ **Friends:** Your Friends Timeline

> ▶ **Mentions:** Tweets directed to you or mentioning you

> ▶ **Messages:** Tweets sent privately to you

> ▶ **Settings:** Preferences for Twittelator

> ▶ **More:** Additional options, features, and Twitter utilities

From the menu, select Settings to set up your Twittelator preferences.

4. The first two options offer a number of tweets received.

> ▶ **Load This Many Tweets:** This feature launches initially however many tweets you select. Then on refreshing, whatever number you select are added to the list of unread tweets.

> ▶ **Search This Many Tweets:** Select from the offered menu how many tweets you want to load after a query.

Set up your options and then scroll down to Reading Tweets options.

FIGURE 10.3 At the bottom of Twittelator's interface is your menu, offering access to your Friends Timeline, Mentions, Direct Messages, App Settings, and additional Twitter features.

NOTE

When Twittelator loads up tweets that you have not seen yet, the icons (as shown in Figure 10.3) are labeled with a small, red alert notifying you how many unread tweets you have.

---

5. Twittelator's Reading Tweets offer the following options:

▶ **Large Font:** You can activate this feature to increase the size of Twittelator's display font.

▶ **Read Newest to Oldest:** Reverse your feed so that the recent posts appear at the bottom of the screen and the older tweets appear at the top.

▶ **Just Screen Name:** Twitter users display by Username and Twitter client.

> ▶ **Open Links in Safari:** This makes URLs in tweets active or inactive.

Set your preferences and continue through your options.

6. The next few groups are specific to composing your tweets:

> ▶ **Writing Tweets:** Preferences specific to help you create tweets.

> ▶ **ReTweet:** Options offered for formatting retweets.

> ▶ **Link Shortening Services:** Choose the URL condenser you prefer to use, if offered.

> ▶ **Photo Serve and Image Options:** Choose both the media sharing service you prefer to share photos on and decide if you want to view high-resolution images.

Set your preferences and scroll down to Autorefresh Tweets options.

7. One of Twittelator Pro's biggest appeals as an iPhone client is its capability to automatically retrieve your tweets. In the Autorefresh Tweets options, set up Twittelator Pro to retrieve tweets at your desired time intervals.

WARNING

Activating Twittelator options makes the app work harder. The harder Twittelator Pro works, the more battery power you consume. Disabling some of the higher functions can conserve battery life, but regardless you will go through an iPhone's battery considerably faster the more you tweet.

---

8. Scroll to the top of your list of tweets and touch the Refresh icon (a circular arrow) at the top of your tweets. This retrieves new tweets.

You can explore some of the other preferences featured here; but with these basics taken care of, it's time to tweet.

Tweeting in Twittelator Pro

1. If you are not in Twittelator Pro viewing either Friends or Mentions, launch Twittelator Pro. On launching the client, you are automatically taken to your Friends timeline.

2. Touch the name of someone (not his avatar) in your Timeline and from the options listed, you can select:

   ▶ **Reply** for the standard @Reply to a tweet.

   ▶ **Re-Tweet (RT)** for retweeting this selected tweet across your network.

   ▶ **Private** to send a DM to this person.

   ▶ **Favorite Tweet** for making a place for this tweet in your own personal Hall of Fame.

   Tap the Reply option to enter in Twittelator's Compose Tweet mode.

FIGURE 10.4   Tapping on a username in your Friends or Mentions timeline can access a variety of options such as Reply, send a DM, Retweet, and much more.

3. Type up your tweet, adding the hashtag #iPhonetweet at the end of it, and touch the blue Send button in the upper-right corner.

4. Once you are back in your Twitter feed, you can send an open tweet to your network by tapping the Compose Tweet button in the top-right corner. Type your tweet, adding the hashtag #twitterin10 at the end of it, and touch the blue Send button in the upper-right corner.

NOTE

Turn your iPhone either to left or right to view the screen in Landscape mode. You note the Compose Tweet mode compensates and now enables you to type using a landscape-oriented keypad, making tweet composition that much easier. You also have available all the terrific add-ons you can give a tweet such as media incorporation, Current Location, and Add Special Characters (also known in typographical circles as Dingbats).

---

5. Tap the Compose Tweet button in the top-right corner again. Before composing your tweet, tap the @ button in the top-right corner. This accesses your Friends list, the users you follow on Twitter. The first 20 names are Recent friends or users you have sent tweets to. Tapping any of the letters along the right side scrolls you down your list of Friends to that letter. Find a user's name you want to tweet and tap that name. You return to the Compose Tweet mode with the Friend's name in place.

6. Type up your tweet. *Do not send this tweet right now.*

NOTE

If you are in need of special characters (vowels with accents, alphanumeric characters specific to a language, and so on), tap-and-hold the letter that is the base of the special character (for example, a vowel, c, ñ, €, or ¿). The options for that letter appear. Drag your finger or thumb to the desired option and release to incorporate it into your tweet.

---

7. Across the bottom of the composition field, you might see Reply to @(username) in gray. Tap that notification once to make the tweet a private message (DM) to that user. Tap it again to make it a reply once more.

8. Type up your tweet, adding the hashtag #twittelator at the end of it, and touch the blue Send button in the top-right corner.

Twittelator Pro does not stop here in the features and functions it offers users. With only a few taps, you can switch from one account to another, keeping track of traffic not only on your primary account but also any other Twitter account you manage.

Multiple Account Setup in Twittelator Pro

1. After purchase, download, and installation, launch Twittelator Pro and then tap the More option, as shown in Figure 10.5, to access additional features and utilities built into Twittelator Pro.

2. Touch your current username (marked with a key icon) at the top of the list.

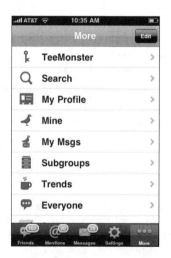

FIGURE 10.5 Twittelator Pro offers you the capability to float between different Twitter accounts, review Trends, perform a variety of Searches, and even set up Subgroups, all with the More option.

3. Touch the Add Account button in the lower-center portion of your interface to add in details of a second Twitter account. Touch Done to complete the login. You now have a new account added to Twittelator. Touch the account you want to monitor.

> **NOTE**
>
> Why have more than one Twitter account? If you decide to run a second Twitter account for your home business, or are recruited to head up a Social Media initiative at your day job, the advantages of a second account become clear. For one thing, the professional account might be a better place to talk shop whereas the personal account can be reviews of **EUReKA** or **Warehouse 13**. Depending on your intent for being on Twitter, you might find the need for a second (third, or more...) account essential.

4. Click on the Friends icon to return to your Friends Timeline.

There is still a great deal more you can do with Twittelator Pro, particularly if you have the iPhone that now features video. With its compact, options-rich U.I., Twittelator Pro brings many of the popular options of applications such as Twhirl and TweetDeck to your iPhone.

Additional Options for Tweets

1. Launch Twittelator Pro. After tweets have loaded, review your feed.

2. Tap the Compose Tweet option to compose a tweet, or tap a username in your feed to reply to another user.

3. After you compose a tweet here, either enter in a URL or paste from your iPhone clipboard a URL copied from Safari. (Disregard the character count.) Tap the Send button. As pictured in Figure 10.6, you have options for shortening the URL or sending the tweet. Tap Shorten Links Then Edit to shorten your link with the Shorten URL service you chose under Settings. You can then edit your tweet, if needed.

4. At the end of the tweet, tap the # in the lower-right portion of the composition field. You should see a scroll wheel of the hashtags you previously used. Scroll to the hashtag you want to add to your tweet and press the blue plus sign (+), or tap the composition window to exit the hashtags mode.

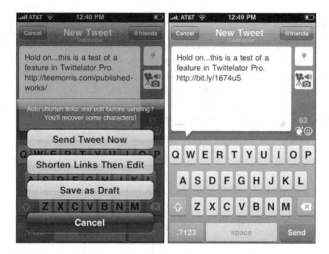

FIGURE 10.6 To shorten a URL in Twittelator Pro, simply enter in the full URL and tap Send to access your URL Shortener of choice (left). You can then return to the tweet to edit it further (right).

5. Now tap on the icon featuring various media (film, audio, photo) located to the right of the composition field. You have all the options available to upload to the media sharing service of your choice. For this exercise, we use photos.

WARNING

While Record Video is offered here, remember that this feature is unavailable unless you have the 3GS iPhone.

---

6. Tap Take Snapshot to take a picture just as you would with your iPhone camera. When you enter Preview mode, select either Retake (left button) to take the photo again or Use (right button) to use that photo. The media icon then represents what you just photographed.

NOTE

When taking pictures live as described in step 6, the new photo is not stored on your camera but uploaded immediately to the media sharing site you choose in your settings as soon as you send the tweet.

---

7. Tap the Send button to share the media with your network. You receive notification as to when the media is uploaded. Tap OK to resume tweeting.

NOTE

If you choose a service such as TwitPic as your default media sharing site, but attempt to send either audio or video, that service automatically switches to MobyPicture because Moby supports more than just images. Find out more about MobyPicture and the various media and formats it supports in Chapter 5, "Incorporating Media with Twitter."

---

8. Tap one of your Friends' *avatars* in your window of tweets. This accesses User Details. (If there is more than one user mentioned in the tweet, you will be asked which user details you want to review.) This window includes user's bio, number of tweets, timeline, network size, Favorites, various follow options, and other details including a detailed look at the user's avatar. Return to Twitter by tapping the Done button at the top-right corner.

Now comes the time for you to explore. The best place to play in Twittelator is under the More option in which many amazing features remain only a finger tap away. Here we take a look at a selling point for Twittelator Pro: The TweetDeck-inspired Subgroups Option.

Creating Subgroups in Twittelator Pro

1. Tap the More option to take a look at the additional options available in Twittelator Pro. Tap the Subgroups option. This is Twittelator Pro's version of TweetDeck's Groups feature. Click on the plus sign (+) at the bottom of the screen to add a new group.

2. From this window, as shown in Figure 10.7, name your group and then add in a name by either typing in a username or scrolling through the people you follow and tap the Add button to the right.

NOTE

If you need the Search mode or your network's scroll wheel but have the keyboard in front of you, simply click the Done button in the lower-right corner of the keyboard. This returns you to the name scroll interface.

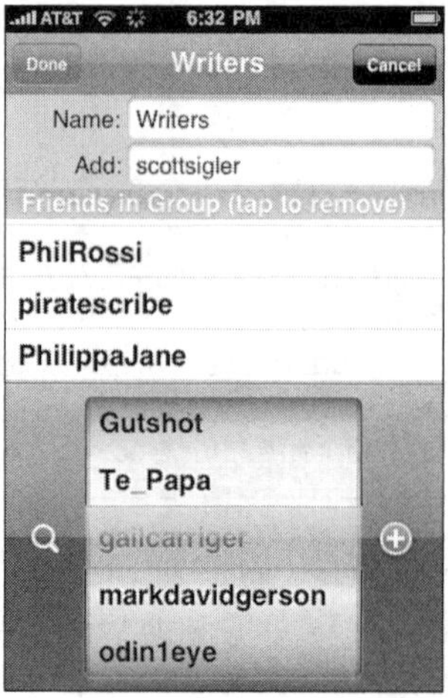

FIGURE 10.7   In the same vein as TweetDeck, Twittelator Pro offers you the ability to organize your network into categories under the More > Subgroups feature.

3. Tap the Search icon (magnifying glass) to the left of your network's scroll wheel, and you access users in the familiar, easy-to-scan Contacts format.

4. When you finish compiling your subgroup, tap the Done button in the upper-left corner. This saves your group.

5. To create a different subgroup, repeat steps 1–4.

6. Tap the group of choice and Twittelator creates a feed featuring only the members of that subgroup. You can switch to your Friends timeline, @Mentions, or DMs; your Subgroup feed remains accessible and active under the More option.

Although there are many, many more features in Twittelator Pro, there is only so much that we cover here. Twittelator is time (and money) well spent. Any closer to the desktop experience and you would be on TweetDeck working Twitter like a pro. Twittelator Pro is a wise investment considering everything it offers you and its stability on the iPhone.

LESSON 11

Building and Rating Your Twitter Network

We have been working throughout the book getting you set up and effectively running like a true Power Twitter, but we actually haven't begun to look into the how's of building a strong, influential network.

Along with Twitter.com suggesting a variety of ways to invite people to Twitter, find Friends, and even follow some interesting people already on the network, many online services cater to the Twitter community with tools designed for account management and to help you seek out other Twitter users that share common interests with you. We now explore the "social" part of Social Networking, reaching out to people on the network and introducing ourselves. Although there is a sense of anonymity here, remember that you deal with real people. Unless the account you reach out to is a spambot (more about that in this chapter), someone is on the receiving end of your Follow request, manning the keyboard. Keep that in mind as you begin to venture out into the Twittersphere and make contacts.

NOTE

You can take precautions to be identified immediately as a real person. Consider your avatar, you bio, and (most important) your username. Is your bio complete? Is your username a "real" name or something such as TeeM8675309? What is your avatar? The more complete, and the more thought out, your Twitter.com presence is, the less likely you will be confused for a spammer. For more on completing your profile, take a look at Chapter 2, "Completing Your Profile."

Working with Twitter.com to Build Your Network

As seen in Chapter 1, "Introducing Twitter," Twitter.com has you build your network right from the start. At any time, you can access these network-building features by going to the top of your Twitter page and clicking on Find People, which gives you four options:

- ▶ **Find on Twitter**—This search option lets you look for people already on Twitter by username or first and last name.

- ▶ **Find on Other Networks**—This option searches Gmail, Yahoo, and AOL for friends who have accounts already registered with Twitter.

- ▶ **Invite by Email**—If you have an email address, you can invite them onto Twitter from here.

- ▶ **Suggested Users**—This is the offered option you saw at the beginning of your signup, now offering more selections because you have a complete profile. Twitter takes a look at the details of your bio, finds active Twitter accounts, and then makes suggestions. With each one you check, Twitter lets you know who you are following when you click on the Follow button.

Using Twitter as a network-building tool is popular because Twitter features a variety of accounts showing active use. It also connects directly to your homepage and is easy to use. After you begin reaching out to build your network (and start tweeting), it should not take long for people to find you.

But how are these people finding you, seemingly at random? What they are doing, outside of what the Find People link offers; Twitter offers *trends* (topics people talk about and either the keyword or a reoccurring hashtag) that you can click and view at any time.

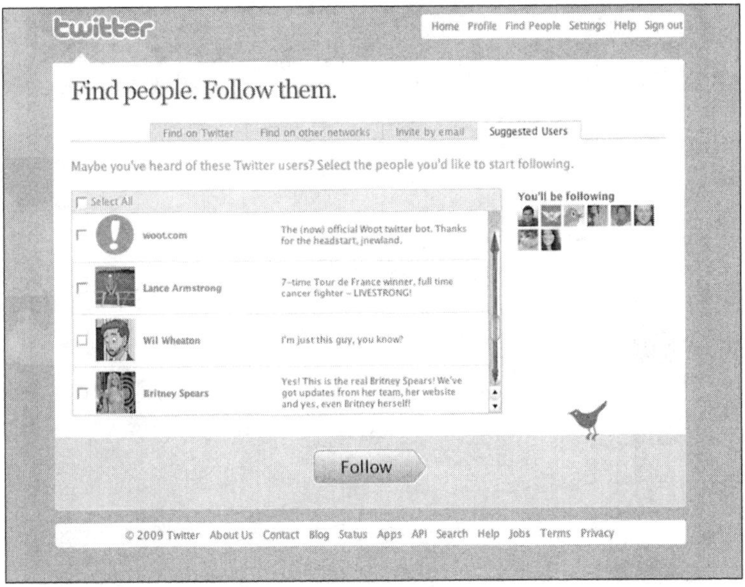

FIGURE 11.1 Your Twitter homepage offers you options under Find People to help you build up your network.

Following Someone at Random on Twitter

1. Go to your Twitter.com homepage, and scroll down (if needed) to view the top Trending Topics in the right column. Click on a term that strikes an interest or curiosity. This shows you the public timeline of everyone on Twitter.

2. Scroll along the first page. If you find a tweet that strikes your interest, click on the username. Twitter immediately sends you to that user's homepage.

3. Look over that first page of tweets. If this Twitter sounds like someone you want to connect with, go to step 4. Otherwise, click on the Home link at the top of the page and repeat steps 1 and 2.

4. Under the user's avatar is a button that says Follow. Click on it.

FIGURE 11.2   Trending Topics appear in your Twitter.com homepage and produce real-time search results for that topic.

WARNING

As seen in Figure 11.2, some Tracking Trends results may not be what you're looking for. Review tweets carefully when using Trending Topics. Spammers are getting more and more creative, masquerading as real people. Although Twitter tries to keep up and close down these bogus accounts, they are out there. Take a moment and review users carefully.

Congratulations! You just made your first random connection on Twitter. This is Social Networking at its easiest and at its finest. To find out more about following people you know are on Twitter or following someone back, review "Building Your Network" in Chapter 2.

NOTE

If you are viewing a follow request in a mail program that does not load web images, you get a text version of this email with active URLs. To visit profiles, simply click the URL to the profile or copy it. You can then launch your browser of choice and paste the URL from the email into the URL field.

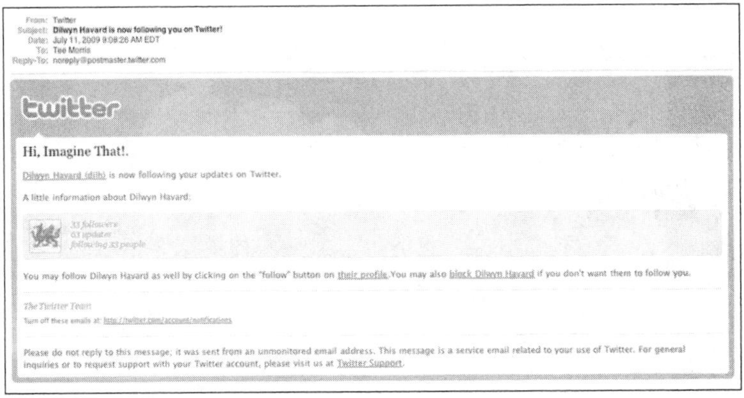

FIGURE 11.3   When someone follows you, Twitter notifies you with an email that gives quick details on your account and options to follow or block.

Using Twitter's homepage is just one way of building your network numbers. There are many other approaches, some of which have already been mentioned in this book, that you can employ.

Using Twitter Search to Build Your Network

Mentioned in Chapter 4, "Tracking Trends and Traffic on Twitter," Twitter Search (http://search.twitter.com) can be used along with another tracking tool—hashtags—to find more users sharing interests in common.

1. Go to http://search.twitter.com and in the empty data field type a term you want to search for in the Public Timeline. Single-click on the Search button.

2. After your search results come in, take a look at the results. You note that although you have tweets that feature your search query, you also have active links to Twitter accounts. Click on a username that strikes your interest.

3. As shown in Figure 11.4, clicking on a username in the search results takes you to that person's Twitter homepage. You can then decide, upon review, whether you would like to follow that person.

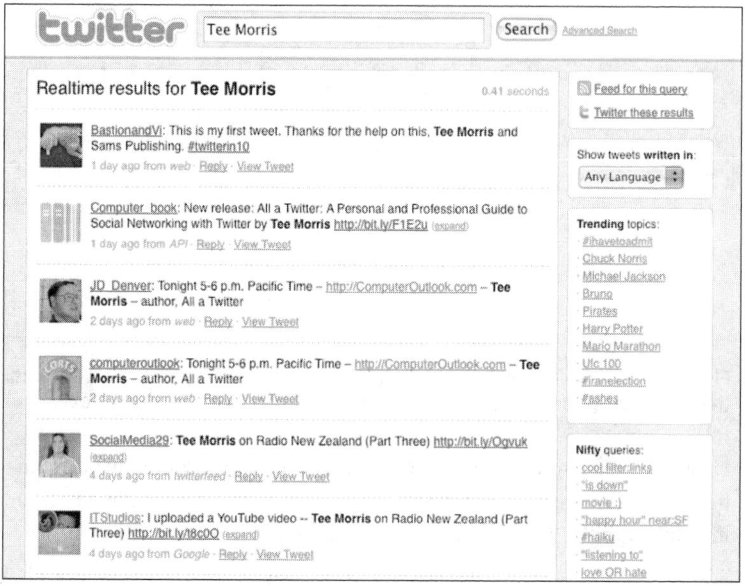

FIGURE 11.4   Twitter Search query results (left) also give active links back to Twitter homepages (right), giving you a list of users who share something in common with you.

NOTE

Remember that you can receive via RSS updates to a search query. To find out more on how to do this, see Chapter 4.

---

4. In the top bar where you see the Twitter logo, enter in a new search but this time enter in a hashtag. You can either find a

popular term from your homepage's Trending Topics or from http://hashtags.org. Enter this as your search term for even more precise results.

As Twitter Search can keep you in the know of what people talk about in your circles of interest, this search engine can also help you bring more people of common interests and likes into your network.

Twitter Search, while a terrific tool for building a network, is not necessarily going to pattern a search based on your interests or even on your previous tweets. There are, though, websites designed to consider all the details of a Twitter account—a bio, your tweets, your current network, and your statistics—that scan the network for people that would make a good match.

Say hello to your online Personal Networking Assistant, Mr. Tweet.

Using Mr. Tweet to Build Your Network

Designed for Twitters who want to build their network fast and efficiently (but without using bots or questionable recruiting tactics) or maybe for new users who are in search of people sharing opinions and outlooks similar to their own, *Mr. Tweet* (pictured in Figure 11.5 and found at http://mrtweet.net) heads out into the Twitterverse and finds others that share opinions, likes, and interests. It's your on-call specialist dedicated to making your Twitter better, stronger, faster.

Starting with Mr. Tweet

Mr. Tweet sets itself apart from other networking services in that the site does not ask for any passwords or usernames initially. Instead Mr. Tweet asks you to follow him. That's the only request. Based on your archived tweets, your participation, and your network, Mr. Tweet notifies you either with a Direct Message (DM) or an email update. Connecting with others from that point is up to you.

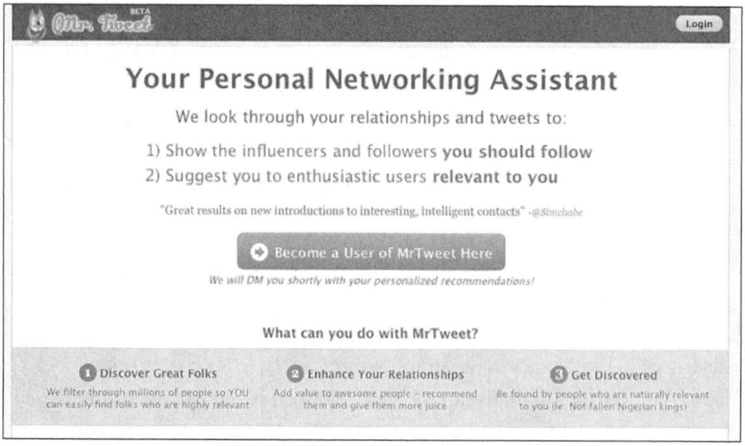

FIGURE 11.5 Mr. Tweet puts the "work" into networking by looking online for Twitter users like you.

1. Go to http://mrtweet.net and click on the "Become a User of Mr. Tweet Here" button.

Also featured here are endorsements, a breakdown of Mr. Tweet's features, and FAQs. If you are still contemplating the why's and how's of Mr. Tweet, take a look here.

2. After you have approved Mr. Tweet, you can either click the login button in the top-right corner, or keep an eye on your DMs. You will be notified (in the same day, perhaps in a few) when Mr. Tweet has results for you to review. Click on the link provided in the DM, and your browser opens at mrtweet.net a page personalized for you, as shown in Figure 11.6.

3. The top page asks you to give recommendations to random users from your network. The accounts featured under "People you Might Be Interested In" are either recommendations from Mr. Tweet, or accounts that are following you but you are not following back.

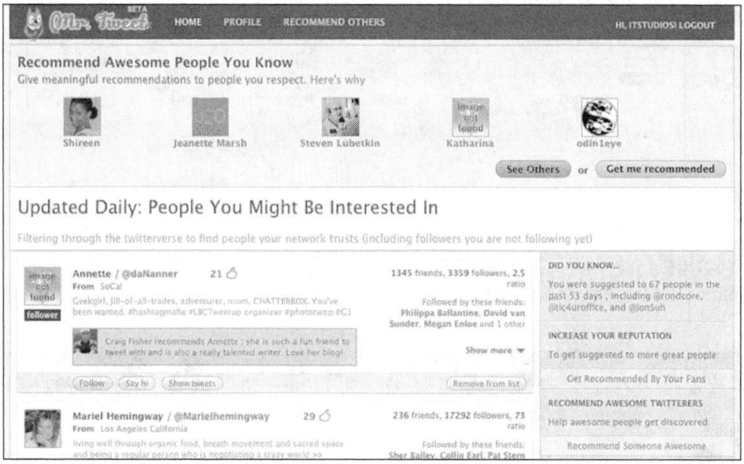

FIGURE 11.6 After creating a profile based on your Archives and public tweets, Mr. Tweet produces a page of relevant Twitters it deduces are good matches.

4. By clicking on the "Show More" option (pictured in Figure 11.7), Mr. Tweet gives you statistics on the Twitter and other users that are connected with this person that you are following.

    From these stats, decide if you want to invite users into your network.

5. Click on the username (usually in blue, preceded by @) to visit a person's Twitter homepage. You can decide if you want to follow that user. You can also click the "Follow" button from the Mr. Tweet page to follow that user.

6. Clicking on the Profile link, pictured in Figure 11.8, is your profile breakdown. These are *your* statistics alongside your profile in Mr. Tweet, an assessment of how you use Twitter from a user standpoint, how engaging you are, and how hard you work to connect others with outside resources.

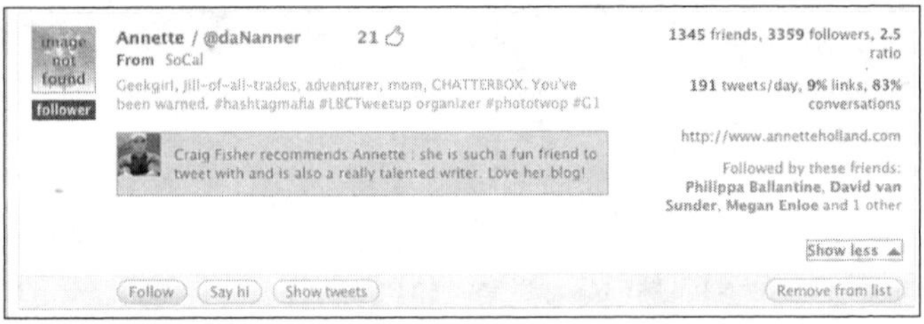

FIGURE 11.7 Mr. Tweet's results include a breakdown of average replies, link exchanges, and updates for these recommended Twitter users.

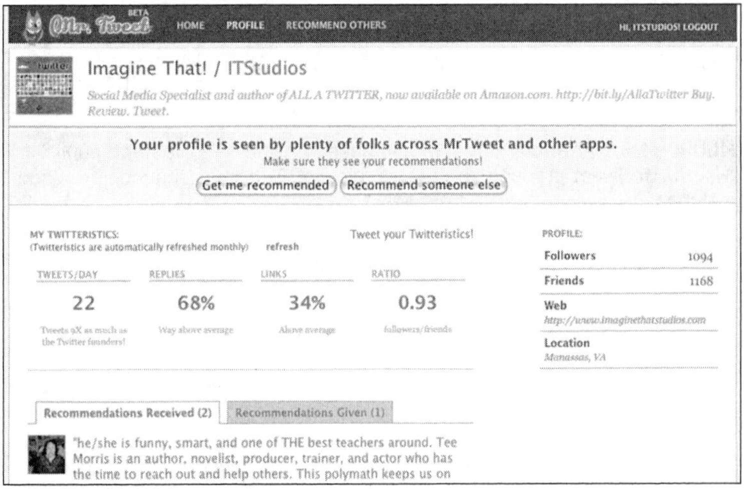

FIGURE 11.8 How do you hold up in the Twitterverse? Mr. Tweet tells you straight up how you measure in your interaction with a Profile breakdown.

7. Scrolling down this page, you can also review recommendations or make recommendations yourself. These are 140-character versions of the endorsements you would find on LinkedIn (http://www.linkedin.com) in which you give a quick nod to a colleague or someone you admire on Twitter. Your recommendation is then sent out to your network, and Mr. Tweet notifies you.

Mr. Tweet can work with you to help screen potential members of your network, build on your Followers, and even improve your network habits.

> **NOTE**
>
> Between the writing of *All a Twitter* and *Sams Teach Yourself Twitter in 10 Minutes*, Mr. Tweet is now working with your account directly as do other services like 12seconds.tv and TwitPic. While Mr. Tweet is a safe service to do this with, do make sure to check with other Twitter users and online about the safety and legitimacy of certain sites. Passwords, at all costs, should be protected.

This website is one of many evaluation services geared to help build your network and improve your Twitter tendencies. These tools are here to help you not only improve your network but also help you to make the most of your 140 characters.

Working with Twitalyzer

Another Twitter assessment service that dedicates itself to not only give you an honest look at how you're tweeting but also goes into how you can improve on your Twitter habits is Twitalyzer (found online at http://www.twitalyzer.com/ and pictured in Figure 11.9).

> **WARNING**
>
> Please note that the service featured here is Twitalyzer, NOT TwitterAnalyzer (http://twitteranalyzer.com). TwitterAnalyzer, although offering an assessment of your account, also practices spamming techniques such as creating bogus Twitter accounts that do nothing but tweet about its services.

Your Twitter account is reviewed and then broken into five categories:

- ▶ **Influence**—This is your impact on Twitter.

- ▶ **Signal-to-Noise Ratio**—Signal-to-Noise (or S:N) goes into the quality of your tweets against their quantity. The quality of what you tweet is assessed by how people react to them, and that goes into the S:N assessment. The higher the quality of tweets, the stronger your signal is. If, however, your tweets are unresponsive, people are tuning you out, regarding your tweets as noise.

- ▶ **Generosity**—Twitalyzer defines Generosity as how much you are sharing (or retweeting) others, passing along in your network links, opinions, and advice and creating within *your* network awareness of the works of others.

WARNING

Twitalyzer states in its definition of Generosity that **"Incidentally, if you retweet more frequently, you'll also increase your signal-to-noise ratio as well...."** Perhaps, but not in the direction you would think. Simply regurgitating other tweets increases the noise in your Twitter S:N. Show that you have your own resources, your own thoughts, and share them on Twitter.

- ▶ **Velocity**—As you might guess, this is how often you tweet. Influential Twitter users tweet often to stay in the loop of discussion and keep their network in the know. If you tweet simply to keep your velocity stat high, though, that can work against you as Followers tune you out.

- ▶ **Clout**—This is Twitalyzer's measure of *Tweet Cred* as determined by traffic *outside* your account. The more people who reference you by account name (@TeeMonster or @ITStudios for myself), the higher your clout.

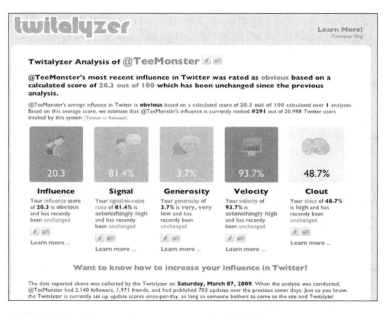

FIGURE 11.9 After entering a username into Twitalyzer, your account is assessed on several characteristics that affect your presence in the Twitter community.

The developers keep the interface simple and (most important) safe and secure.

1. Go to http://twitalyzer.com and enter your Twitter username in the text field provided.

WARNING

The problem you have with TweetStats and protected updates also applies with Twitalyzer. Twitalyzer does not work with protected updates.

2. Single-click the Twitalyze! button. Your account is assessed, and then your results appear on your browser.

3. Click on any of the pencil icons associated with a category to send your results across your network as a tweet.

4. Over time, you can return to Twitalyzer, repeat steps 1–2, and then scroll down for progress analysis and compare-and-contrast with other Twitters using Google Motion Charts.

Twitalyze is more than just an honest assessment of your Twitter account, but its real influence comes after you make return visits to assess growth. The comparison tools, not only against yourself over time but also with other Twitters, can give you goals and benchmarks, making your accounts more productive and your community all the stronger.

Why Automated Services Are a Bad Idea

Particularly in business, it's all about the numbers. In April 2009, Ashton Kutcher reduced Twitter to a numbers game opposite of CNN. For the self-proclaimed Social Media Gurus, Mavens, and Experts, you're truly nobody on Twitter unless you have the numbers behind you.

However, you have to stop and ask:

▶ How did these people get these numbers?

▶ Did they truly review and approve these users?

▶ Are these people actually paying attention to their network?

▶ How effectively are they networking across such a vast amount of Followers?

Perhaps the bigger question here is "Can you have too large of a network?" The answer to that rests in what kind of Twitter presence you want to establish. If you want something personal, the peace of mind that at least—at one point—you physically reviewed a Follower's homepage, made a judgment call, and followed that person, then amassing the massive numbers will not happen overnight for you. Neither will maintaining real, tangible connections with your network. The larger your Followers become, the harder it will be to maintain an accurate track on your feed. When the growth is gradual, however, it is easier to establish ties and cultivate relationships, both on a professional and personal level.

> **WARNING**
>
> In many instances, sites that promise you followers like TweeterFollow.com and GatherFollowers.com will, on getting your username and password, spam your networking using **your** feed. When asked for your password, make sure you're at a site that offers quality services and not incessant spam.

It is when that community you want to nurture jumps from 1,000 Followers to 10,000 to 100,000 overnight that your entire approach to Twitter changes. If your presence on Twitter becomes nothing more than inspirational quotes, retweets, and promotions for your own business, you will be tuned out by people that suddenly find themselves following you. This is the cost of shortcuts. There is a lot of security in knowing your community, in building it without implementing the shortcut. Unsupervised growth turns your Twitter account as a means of broadcasting to your clientele. Business as usual. Throwing a message out to the great unknown to see if it sticks. This is a poor choice to make concerning Social Networking and a worse one when attempting to build a community.

> **WARNING**
>
> Twitter users who joined Twitter for its networking potential and social aspect are also stepping up and taking stands against these services that inflate accounts with Followers. Many on receiving messages featuring URLs promising new Followers are unfollowing these users. Some are outright blocking them.
>
> And then there's codemonkey, designer, author, speaker, blogger, swordfighter (gulp!), and all-around, in-your-face, boot-on-the-trachea funny woman, Alison Gianotto (@snipeyhead), who goes one step further: She mocks them.
>
> In a salvo that rivals the sinking of the **Bismark**, Gianotto takes aim at the developers behind the automated Twitter developers, the self-proclaimed Social Media oracles endorsing these services, and those blindly buying what all of the above are selling and satirizes them in The Complete Social Media Douchebag (http://socialmedi-adouchebag.net, as shown in Figure 11.10). From the name you can

be assured this is a website not for the kids nor for the faint-of-heart, but with a razor-sharp, Monty Python-esque delivery, this site manages to point out "business practices" on Twitter that have managed to alienate users worldwide.

This hysterical website is merely the tip of the iceberg when it comes to the automated approach to Twitter. Make certain you and your business are not on the **Titanic** when launching your own Social Media initiative.

FIGURE 11.10 Automated Twitter services have not only brought on the wrath of those in the Twitterverse (as shown at this website), but from Twitter itself.

Another reason to avoid the automated services for building your network is its latest opponent: Twitter.

In the June 19, 2009, ReadWriteWeb blogpost "Dear Wanna-bes, Your Twitter Stardom is Coming to an End" (http://bit.ly/AutoTwitter), Twitter's own Doug Williams commented on software and online sites systematically adding connections each day only to break those connections with anyone not reciprocating. "There is no limit to the number of unfollows," he states. "Using software to constantly churn Followers in a repeated pattern of following and unfollowing will however risk suspension." Strong words. It was not made clear in the article or on Twitter's own blog when this crackdown would occur; but because it has the attention of Twitter, it is only a matter of time.

Twitter is not about the shortcuts but about the sincerity. Although you can make no claims that you can truly know all your Followers on Twitter, you can say without question that you visit every page, review tweets, and made a judgment call to follow or not follow someone. It is about being discerning about who you want to engage, and whether the user in question is a positive or negative influence.

It's what The Doctor once said: "A straight line may be the shortest distance between two points, but it is by no means the most interesting." There is something to be said in knowing—really knowing—who is in your network. Creating the community without shortcuts might take longer, but in the end your network will be built on a stronger ethic of quality rather than quantity.

Twitter Twoubleshooting

The greatest fear at the end of any book is that feeling of what you do if you do not find what you are looking for. After all, you picked up this book for answers, and perhaps in the bookstore you went through the index and found the answer to one of your questions. But then you are hitting a brick wall, whatever issue plaguing you on Twitter still nowhere closer to resolution, or worse—closer to a resolution you would like to see.

I have been there myself. Many times. And I am confident enough to say "Don't worry—I know a guy who knows a guy…." This is the "Break Glass in Case of Emergency" chapter that gives you recommendations on where to find help with Twitter when you're having one of *those* days online.

Support from Twitter.com

Twitter has worked to be as self-sufficient as possible, offering several options all hosted at Twitter's website. These are the voices of its creators, and its community, offering insight, opinion, and commentary on what is happening at Twitter and what direction the traffic is taking them.

Twitter Support

Accessed by simply going to the top of your Twitter homepage and clicking the Help link, Twitter Support (http://help.twitter.com) starts with answering the most basic of questions: How do I use Twitter? Their answer is a 4-minute video from Howcast (http://www.howcast.com) that takes you through the basics of Twitter from setting up an account to sending out a tweet.

Following this fantastic orientation video, Twitter Support breaks down into the following sections:

▶ **Please, help yourself…**—This is the "Self Service" of Twitter. First, a Known Issues link takes you to an online forum hosted by Twitter, providing users a place to post issues and reoccurring problems. Then there is the Status Blog that is discussed later in this chapter.

▶ **Using Help Resources**—These are a collection of links taking you throughout Twitter's network of forums, assistance blogs, and various online resources outlining policies and terms of service.

▶ **Want to contribute?**—Here, Twitter invites you the user to contribute your own article, video, or insight into making Twitter a better experience for the network.

FIGURE 12.1   Twitter Support is your first step in trying to find the answers to the unanswerable issues in Twitter.

Twitter Support might seem to be a rehash of what you find in this book, but you might find something straight from the home site that didn't get covered anywhere in this book. Twitter Support is, like many of the recommendations made here, a different perspective on issues both common and uncommon.

Twitter Blog

If you want the inside scoop and even an open honesty in what is going on at Twitter, another valuable resource is the Twitter Blog found at http://blog.twitter.com. The voice at Twitter Blog is described as open because the blog posts, coming directly from Biz Stone of Twitter, are brutally honest both in favor of and criticizing Twitter.

On July 15, 2009, Twitter experienced a severe security breach (http://bit.ly/TwitterSecurity). Biz Stone did not hide behind rhetoric or even deny the claims of Twitter debacle. Instead, Biz stepped up and openly admitted that there was a screw-up, assured users that accounts were safe and sound, and addressed the lessons learned and new procedures founded to avoid something like this happening again.

FIGURE 12.2   To hear one of the founders of Twitter sound off on what is happening at homepage, simply take a look (and subscribe) to Twitter Blog.

The range of topics vary on Twitter Blog. There is news ranging from new SMS coverage for international mobile carriers to various applications of Twitter. You might find notifications on changes concerning your Twitter.com homepage layout. Twitter Blog is Step Two in working with Twitter.com to find your answers, but it is also your inside look at how Twitter is handling its growth, its network, and its future.

Twitter Status

The last place Twitter offers to give you a head's up on how things are going back at homebase is Twitter Status (http://status.twitter.com), a blog that is not open for comments but is more of a delivery device similar to Status Updates found in both Twhirl and TweetDeck (both can be found in Chapters 6, "Using Third-Party Applications: Twhirl," and 7, "Using Third-Party Applications: TweetDeck"). Twitter Status keeps users informed on any scheduled or sudden outages in the network, including improvements for data networks and mobile carriers that work with Twitter to make Twitter-to-Go faster and more effective.

If you suddenly find yourself without Twitter, but the rest of your Internet connections are up and running, review Twitter Status to see if everything is okay on the operations level. If there is an outage or planned maintenance, you can find a notice here.

> **NOTE**
>
> Click on the Pingdom Uptime Report link in the right sidebar, and you can take a look at a monthly average of when Twitter was online, offline, and its response time.

These are all the various ways you can monitor your Twitter account and ask for help on matters beyond this book. If, however, you still can't find the answer to what you are looking for from Twitter, there is always the Internet. Remember though that the people in the wilds of cyberspace are not affiliated with Twitter. They are the users, free of the constraints of Twitter's website and making their own judgment calls and drawing their own conclusion as to why Twitter is doing what it is doing.

They might not have an inside track, but they do offer a user's perspective to Twitter, different from both this book and Twitter.com, making them good resources to know about.

Blogs and Podcasts Concerning Twitter

Perhaps these websites are not officially endorsed or recognized by Twitter, but these online information havens are valuable because they bring in a fresh point-of-view to the Social Networking service. Some of these sites report Twitter in the news, peppering the story with their own commentary. Others give an overview of what is happening in the Twitterverse. Whatever information you find, technical or trivial, you can find out something new about Twitter from these users who bring their own experiences to you.

Mashable.com

Founded in 2005 by Pete Cashmore, Mashable is the world's largest blog covering all Social Media matters, reporting the breaking stories on Social Media resources and the latest trends. It pulls in millions of page views per month and is cited often within the blogosphere, the podosphere, Facebook, and (of course) Twitter.

FIGURE 12.3 Mashable, arguably the best news source for all things Social Media, keeps Twitter users in the know on developments and breaking news concerning Social Networking.

Part of Mashable's appeal is its unabashed viewpoint of what is happening in Social Media. An example of this can be seen in the earlier cited news story of July 15, 2009, when Twitter suffered a major failure in its security. Mashable's Stan Schroeder added to the report on the incident the following:

> One thing is certain. Twitter needs to **burn** everything security-related **down to the ground** and build it all anew to make sure this won't happen again. Employees should adopt stricter security practices; services that don't offer adequate security should be replaced with better ones; in short, Twitter needs to seriously **rethink its attitude towards security** and privacy in all aspects of their work.

Mashable.com and its commentary-peppered news reporting make it something like Social Media's answer to CNN's *The Situation Room*. If you are looking to keep an eye on trends and the latest news concerning Twitter, Mashable.com is a resource you should have in your RSS reader.

TechCrunch

If Mashable is *The Situation Room* of Social Media news, TechCrunch (http://www.techcrunch.com) could best be described as *The Daily Show*. Founded in 2005, and now a massive network of blogs all covering all things tech, TechCrunch is dedicated to profiling and reviewing emerging Internet products and companies, and profiling existing companies that make an impact in Social Networks.

TechCrunch reports the news on what is happening with Twitter, but it doesn't mind slipping in some jaded commentary. Even in some of its titles (that is, No, @Oprah doesn't really want you to watch that pirated copy of Harry Potter; Another Security Tip For Twitter: Don't Use "Password" As Your Server Password), it is clear that TechCrunch offers a fair amount of sarcasm in its news reporting.

FIGURE 12.4 TechCrunch provides (with a healthy dose of snark) headlines and commentary on all things online.

ReadWriteWeb

From the land of the Long White Cloud comes ReadWriteWeb (http://read-writeweb.com), a blog that has provided Web Technology news, reviews, and analyses since 2003. This is where you go when you want your latest developments concerning Social Media free of the more opinionated approaches Mashable and TechCrunch are famous for. ReadWriteWeb is now one of the most widely read and respected blogs in the world, first started by Richard MacManus and is now manned by a writing team dedicated to the web-centric technology, ranked by Technorati in its Top 20 most popular blogs worldwide and one of the Top 10 of Techmeme's Leaderboard.

ReadWriteWeb goes beyond the realms of Social Media, also reporting on developments at Google, Microsoft, and Apple. There is also a terrific crossover between articles concerning traditional media (print, television, radio) and how it attempts to integrate new media practices (blogs, podcasts, and such). This is a blog dedicated to reporting the news, reserving its own commentary but presenting all sides of an issue and leaving you—the reader—to comment with your own opinion and conclusions. Consider ReadWriteWeb when you need your perspective on Social Media snark-free, de-opinionated, and sticking to just the facts.

FIGURE 12.5   A long-time resource for all things happening on the web, ReadWriteWeb gives a polished, balanced report and commentary on Internet news.

Twooting

From the podosphere, there are several offerings, both of the professionally polished and off-the-cuff approach to Twitter. *Twooting* (http://twooting.com), hosted by Bo Bennett and Ryan Levesque, is where "Twitter means business." Bo and Ryan offer their own commentary on Twitter in the news, review various third-party utilities geared for Twitter users, host interviews of personal and professional Twitter users, and broaden their discussion to Twitter's impact on the Internet. Twooting went live in March 2009, and creates content on a frequent level, better than some Twitter podcasts that have already come and gone. Take a listen to Twooting for all Twitter topics, all the time.

FIGURE 12.6 Podcasts (such as Word on the Tweet, pictured here) give fresh perspectives, Twitter headlines, and commentary on Twitter topics.

Word on the Tweet

If Twooting is *Siskel and Ebert: At the Movies*, then *Word on the Tweet* (http://www.wordonthetweet.net) is the Twitterverse's *Meet the Press*. Hosts Jeff Parsons and Fred Abaroa invite other Twitter users on their show to discuss the Trending Topics on Twitter alongside other developments in Social Media and its impact on Twitter. Parsons and Abaroa allow the show to discuss other tangents that the Trending Topics lead to. In the midst of this informality, Word on the Tweet produces a sweet, solid sound (and I'm thinking that is Parsons' background as a Q97.9 radio personality that the podcaster in me loves!), making the close-on-1-hour content very easy to digest.

Social Media Security

A growing issue in Social Media is security. Exactly how safe is all this socializing, how much information are we truly sharing, and what can we do to protect ourselves? For these answers concerning Twitter (and other Social Media initiatives) have a look at the blog and podcast, *Social Media Security* (http://socialmediasecurity.com). Hosted by security experts Scott Wright and Tom Eston, this blog and podcast goes into the technical details of what malicious hacker-types are developing to make Twitter work against you. There are also terrific tips offered in being safe when traversing the Twitterverse.

Tweet Week

Finally, on the video podcasting arena, there is digital geek girl and Twitter aficionado Julia Roy and her one-woman weekly talk show, *Tweet Week* (http://tweetweek.blip.tv/). This is 7 minutes of pure fun, embodying the light-hearted attitude of Twitter. Julia comments on the hottest trends, top tweeted websites, and appearances of Twitter in the news. She also gives her own take on the wittiest, funniest, and downright hysterical tweets that come across her Twitter feed. If you want a down-to-earth and infectiously perky viewpoint on what is happening on the network, sub-scribe to Tweet Week and enjoy the gossip and going on.

These blogs and podcasts are actively (and in some cases, aggressively) producing content geared to help you with Twitter and answer your ques-tions concerning Twitter. These sites and media offerings are only a few of the offerings out there. Searches on Google and iTunes bring up a wide variety of resources that talk not only about Twitter, but also discuss Facebook, MySpace, and so on.

But throughout this book, you have grown to know me and know my voice, my perspective, my opinions. You have grown to trust me and my advice on Twitter. So when this book is over and done with, is there some place online where you can hear me go beyond this book, even beyond my other title, *All a Twitter*?

As a matter of fact….

Bird House Rules

As mentioned in the opening of this title, *Bird House Rules* (reached through http://twitterin10.com) is the official blog and podcast of *All a Twitter* and this book. The blog will be my own reviews and tips on the latest Twitter tools that appear online, any business pertaining to my Twitter titles, and appearances on venues like Computer Outlook (http://www.computeroutlook.com) and Radio New Zealand (http://www.radionz.co.nz). There will also be the occasional reporting of Twitter in the News, featuring links to earlier resources cited here. Commentary I was not allowed in this title you can find at Bird House Rules, but I will continue to keep this title relevant through its many postings.

FIGURE 12.7   From the author of *All a Twitter* and *Sams Teach Yourself Twitter in 10 Minute*s is the companion blog and podcast for both books, Bird House Rules.

Then you have the 10-minute podcast which also picks up where *Sams Teach Yourself Twitter in 10 Minutes* leaves off. Presenting material in both audio and (when the time and the situation allows) video formats, *Bird House Rules* keeps your Twitter Fu current and up-to-date. Its intent is to be your addendum to both *Sams Teach Yourself Twitter in 10 Minutes* and my earlier title, *All a Twitter*. The podcast is also your platform to sound off about something in the book you agreed with, disagreed with, or missed. Have an idea or a topic you'd like to see me discuss? Please, let me know by leaving a comment on the blog or contacting me on Twitter.

Now with the resources in reach, this book close at hand, and everything we have covered from page 1 to now, the rest is up to you. Although I can talk about it in the podcast and within the pages of a Twitter book, no one can be taught participation. You simply have to do it. That level of participation is best gauged by you, and your level of success with Twitter depends on how much you want to invest into your network. If you remember that the best voice to speak with on Twitter and the best judgment to call to make on how you build your network is your own and not some automated service, the Twitter experience can remain a positive and (if you are most fortunate) a profitable one. This title has taken you from the beginning steps, but it does not end here. *Sams Teach Yourself Twitter in 10 Minutes* is the foundation. Now comes the real work, and this is where the potential and the influence of Twitter comes to light. Enjoy the journey, and remain true to your plan for what you want to accomplish. With the right execution and a realistic approach, you can achieve your goals and even surprise yourself with the new ones that will appear on the horizon. All this and more awaits you, in messages 140 characters or less in length.

Welcome to Twitter.

Index

SamsTeachYourself

from Sams Publishing

Sams Teach Yourself in 10 Minutes
offers straightforward, practical answers
for fast results.

These small books of 250 pages or less
offer tips that point out shortcuts and
solutions, cautions that help you avoid
common pitfalls, notes that explain
additional concepts and provide additional
information. By working through the
10-minute lessons, you learn everything
you need to know quickly and easily!

When you only have time for the answers,
Sams Teach Yourself books are your
best solution.

Visit **informit.com/samsteachyourself**
for a complete listing of the products
available.

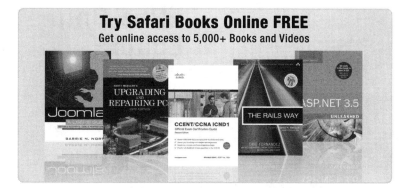

FREE Online Edition

Your purchase of *Sams Teach Yourself Twitter in 10 Minutes* includes access to a free online edition for 45 days through the Safari Books Online subscription service. Nearly every Sams book is available online through Safari Books Online, along with more than 5,000 other technical books and videos from publishers such as Addison-Wesley Professional, Cisco Press, Exam Cram, IBM Press, O'Reilly, Prentice Hall, and Que.

SAFARI BOOKS ONLINE allows you to search for a specific answer, cut and paste code, download chapters, and stay current with emerging technologies.

Activate your FREE Online Edition at www.informit.com/safarifree

> **STEP 1:** Enter the coupon code: IHUZGAA.

> **STEP 2:** New Safari users, complete the brief registration form. Safari subscribers, just log in.

If you have difficulty registering on Safari or accessing the online edition, please e-mail customer-service@safaribooksonline.com